COOK YOUR OWN F*CKING LIFE

VEGAN COMFORT FOOD RECIPES

TO FEED YOURSELF AND BUILD COMMUNITY

ASHLEY ROWE PALAFOX

COOK YOUR OWN FUCKING LIFE

Vegan Comfort Food Recipes to Feed Yourself and Build Community

Part of the DIY Series

First Edition, 2,000 copies, first published November, 2025
ISBN 9781648413926
This is Microcosm # 952
Designed by Sarah Koch
Edited by Lex Orgera

For a catalog, write or visit:

Microcosm Publishing
2752 N Williams Ave.
Portland, OR 97227

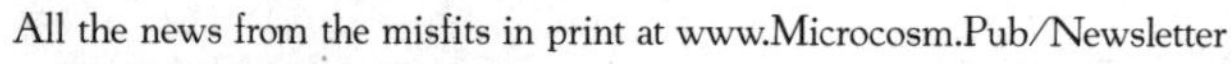
All the news from the misfits in print at www.Microcosm.Pub/Newsletter

Get more copies of this book at www.Microcosm.pub/CookYourOwn

Read more about cooking vegan: www.Microcosm.pub/Cooking

Did you know that you can buy our books directly from us at sliding scale rates? Support a small, independent publisher and pay less than Amazon's price at **www. Microcosm.Pub.**

To join the ranks of high-class stores that feature Microcosm titles, talk to your rep: In the U.S. COMO (Atlantic), ABRAHAM (Midwest), BOB BARNETT (Texas, Oklahoma, Arkansas, Louisiana), IMPRINT (Pacific), TURNAROUND (UK), UTP/MANDA (Canada), NEWSOUTH (Australia/New Zealand), Observatoire (Africa, Europe), IPR (Middle East), Yvonne Chau (Southeast Asia), HarperCollins (India), Everest/B.K. Agency (China), Tim Burland (Japan/Korea), and FAIRE in the gift trade.

Global labor conditions are bad, and our roots in industrial Cleveland in the 70s and 80s made us appreciate the need to treat workers right. Therefore, our books are MADE IN THE USA and printed on post-consumer paper.

EU Safety Information: https://microcosmpublishing.com/gpsr

MICROCOSM PUBLISHING is Portland's most diversified publishing house and distributor, with a focus on the colorful, authentic, and empowering. Our books and zines have put your power in your hands since 1996, equipping readers to make positive changes in their lives and in the world around them. Microcosm emphasizes skill-building, showing hidden histories, and fostering creativity through challenging conventional publishing wisdom with books and bookettes about DIY skills, food, bicycling, gender, self-care, and social justice. What was once a distro and record label started by Joe Biel in a drafty bedroom was determined to be *Publishers Weekly*'s fastest-growing publisher of 2022 and #3 in 2023, and is now among the oldest independent publishing houses in Portland, OR, and Cleveland, OH. Biel is also the winner of PubWest's Innovator Award in 2024. We are a politically moderate, centrist publisher in a world that has inched to the right for the past 80 years.

Contents

The Obligatory (Omnibus) Introduction

This book had its beginnings nearly twenty years ago, in the cramped (and, let's face it, kind of grimy) kitchen of a duplex in Santa Cruz, California. I was living on my own for the first time, joyfully surrounded by the punks and weirdos I felt most at home with and splitting my time evenly between school, shows, and refining any new vegan dish I could come up with. It was this last one, of course, that would inspire the zine *Barefoot and in the Kitchen*, the contents of which make up this book.

As a teenager, the bands I loved most had shaped my politics and guided my ethics toward animal liberation. By twenty years old, I had a few years of veganism under my belt. This was the age of silken-tofu-everything and feeling lucky if you could find one alternative milk option at the store—let alone for your latte. There was content on the internet and, indeed, this is where I picked up some of my most-used cooking techniques. But my favorite plant-based cookbook at the time was from a 1970s hippie commune, and the options for finding recipes were just not yet what they would go on to become, to put it mildly.

I knew cooking could be a chore, but I also realized how fun and liberating it could be to funnel my creativity into the kitchen and be the one responsible for nourishing myself and the folks I loved. I felt inspired by cooking, inventing and perfecting recipes and using new ingredients, often occupying the kitchen for much of the day. I realized quickly that I'd amassed a good amount of tasty and straightforward recipes that other people I knew might want to use. The punk scene with its DIY ethos taught me to share my resources with others; it also taught me that there was nothing stopping me from publishing my ideas myself! So, I typed up the recipes I'd created, drew a cover image, cut up some magazine pages and flyers for a little bit of flare, and gluesticked everything together into my first zine—*Barefoot and in the Kitchen Volume One* was born.

I'd intended this to be something I shared with friends and family who were looking for help feeding the vegans in their lives and had no aspirations for wide distribution. I made twenty-five copies, which were all gone before I knew it. Ok, people were kind of interested in this thing! Off to the copy shop again, then again and again. What followed over the next few years was something I never could have anticipated: three more volumes, and thousands of pages copied, collated, stapled and stuffed into envelopes or piled up on tables at shows and zine events. Like most people who dare to assume their creative efforts will find an audience if only they are brave enough to put them out into the world, I reaped the benefits. I made friends with likeminded people I may never have met without the zine. My cat, GG, who was a kitten when I published the first issue, had life saving surgery a few years later in large part thanks to money I brought in fundraising with *Barefoot.* My friends and I made buttons with his little face on them that said, "I helped a kitty!" and sent them out with the orders, and I will never forget that it was my community who helped me to pay his mountain of vet bills, for a few vegan recipes in return.

Since the zine came out, just about everything in the world of vegan food has changed. I use ingredients now I never would have dreamed of having access to when I was writing *Barefoot,* and I find them in stores I never would have thought might carry them. Vegan food has cycled in and out of trendiness, but it has firmly established its place in the general consciousness, and chances of finding something suitable to eat in any given restaurant are better now than they have ever been, I am certain. The internet overflows with recipes, and the cookbook aisle in the bookstore is flush with options. All this variety owes a debt to the vegans who were on the vanguard before it was in vogue, and I owe my small contribution to the canon to them, too.

In light of all the changes of the last two decades, it feels worthwhile to preserve this work as a sort of time capsule—albeit a functional, living one, far from a mere curiosity. This book presents the contents of the original zines as more than the sum of their parts. It includes more than fifty delicious recipes that I still use in my own kitchen, and that I know you will enjoy. The book also offers a peek into the scene of the early 2000s, when DIY was not just an aesthetic but a necessity in living what would now be called a "plant-based" lifestyle. Veganism was not yet the trend it would become, for both better and worse, and still bore the fangs of its radical politics and countercultural roots.

Looking back on the content from my current vantage point, I've added annotations throughout the book to provide some context and to reflect what's changed—in my thoughts on the recipes (and on food in general) as well as in the world at large—in the years since the zines were first published. The publisher and I have corrected some typos, too, because we couldn't help ourselves.

There are also some notes worth making up front. One is that I reference soy milk a lot in the recipes. You may remember when it was tough to find soy milk, let alone something like oat milk, which we now take for granted, but know that when I say "soy" I now mean any of the fabulous and abundant varieties of non-dairy milks that may be available to you. Take your pick! Same with "soy cheese," as in the potato casserole recipe. We are truly living in the golden era of vegan cheese these days—hallelujah!

Another is that you'll see me say throughout the original zines that I want (and expect!) you to take what I've created as a good, solid base and make it your own. This is something I stand by wholeheartedly and something I wish someone had told me sooner when I was first learning how to cook. Your food is for you—make it how you like! Season it, taste it, and season it again. Love mushrooms? I don't. But you do you, my friend, and add them in where you see fit. Have fun.

If anything, these notes from the present day highlight how *Barefoot and in the Kitchen* embodies a particular moment in time, mirroring the countless self-published artifacts of the punk and underground music scenes of the preceding decades. The California Restaurant Guide section at the back of each volume was very much in the spirit of *Maximum RocknRoll's Book Your Own Fuckin' Life* zine, which guided DIY bands of all stripes to bookers and venues that would welcome them and align with their values. Just as *BYOFL* was updated over the course of its run, the entries in my Restaurant Guide have been annotated to give you, well, information that's accurate and not twenty years old.

In inviting you to Cook Your Own Fucking Life, I like to think I am keeping alive the tradition of helping to create the world you want to inhabit. I hope you'll find some of the same inspiration and satisfaction here that I have, and I hope you'll help hand the torch off to others, too. Resistance is tasty—spread the word.

barefoot
and in the
Kitchen
of our own accord
volume
one ♡
vegan
recipes
for you
↑
from me
(ashley)

VEGAN
DEATH
SQUAD

Innards

the obligatory introduction

Personally, I love being barefoot and in the kitchen. I think it's one of the simple joys in life. I never understood what the negative connotation was (ok, ok, hundreds of years of women's oppression, etc. Yeah, I guess I do understand). Anyway, I want to reclaim the kitchen as a space where work happens because you want it to and enjoy doing it, not because you have to.

I spend a lot of my time in the kitchen, and being vegan, maybe this means more to me than most people. It's a good thing I love cooking because it would be much harder for me to get through the average day if I had to rely on the shit other people prepared all the time. So I make my own. And I love it.

The recipes in this zine are a mix between ones I've developed completely on my own (as in "hey, I miss broccoli soup….gonna have to invent me some vegan broccoli soup!") and a few are adaptations or straight up copies of some you might find elsewhere. I don't give credit to these sources (except for the Farm vegetarian cookbook, because it is seriously worth it!) and I don't really expect credit for my recipes. As long as everyone is making and spreading the love of good vegan food, it's all worth it.

THE CINNAMON BUNS RECIPE IS ACTUALLY THE ONLY ONE IN THIS VOLUME THAT I 'STRAIGHT UP COPIED' FROM SOMEWHERE ELSE. THE FOUNDATIONS OF SOME OTHER RECIPES LIKE THE BASIC SEITAN CAME FROM ONLINE SOMEWHERE, BUT I REWROTE AND ADAPTED THESE AND THEY'RE PROBABLY LONG GONE FROM WHATEVER OLD-SCHOOL WEBSITES I FOUND THEM ON.

THERE IS A CERTAIN PRIVILEGE IN TALKING ABOUT COOKING 'NOT BECAUSE YOU HAVE TO' BECAUSE, OF COURSE, MANY PEOPLE ABSOLUTELY DO HAVE TO. IN THE YEARS SINCE I WROTE THIS, I'VE FOUND MYSELF HAVING TO COOK WHILE WORKING, GOING TO SCHOOL (AND WORKING), AND TAKING CARE OF MYSELF AND OTHERS. DESPITE THE PRIVILEGE IN MY OWN LIFE, I'VE FOUND MYSELF FALLING OUT OF LOVE WITH COOKING AT TIMES WHEN IT BECAME SOMETHING I DID ONLY OUT OF NECESSITY, IN A TIME CRUNCH, WITHOUT AS MUCH EMPHASIS AS I'D LIKE ON THE BEAUTIFUL →

Maybe you're used to those cardboard-tasting, strangely textured, low-fat vegan meals you find in a lot of cookbooks (and restaurants for that matter). And maybe that's what you're looking for. Well, you won't find it here (I hope). These are recipes I want people to be able to feed to meat eaters to show them that not all vegan food tastes like gruel.

That's also what the restaurant guide in the back is all about. These places are just a handful of incredibly vegan and vegan-friendly restaurants in California which I have been to and will personally tell you are worthwhile. They're of all different types and prices and are scattered about, for your convenience (if you're in California at all, that is).

If you have any questions, comments or suggestions about the restaurant list or any other part of the zine, I would love to hear from you. I really would. My contact info is in the back. If you have any recipes I should try, books I should read, or restaurants to include in the next issue, let me know! You can also order more copies or copies of volume two, which will be out soon.

Thanks for picking this up, and I hope you have fun with it. Pick the parts you like and change them so you like them even more! ♡

INSPIRATION POSSIBLE IN THE KITCHEN. BUT! I KNOW THERE IS JOY TO BE FOUND IN COOKING, AND I HOPE TO HELP YOU FIND IT HERE, TOO. THINK OF YOUNG, ENTHUSIASTIC ASHLEY WHEN YOU'RE NOT FEELING IT AND TRY TO GET CREATIVE, EVEN JUST A LITTLE BIT! ♡

2

things you won't find in this cookbook

*quick and easy meals

*suggestions for the use of brown rice, whole wheat flour, etc. (unless you want to use those, which may well be a good idea)

*weight loss tips or helpful low fat recipes (although some happen to be low fat)

*any non-vegan crap, including honey (yes, that counts)

*the recipe to save the world (well, maybe)

*a cute kitten (well, actually, he makes an appearance too)

*professional layout, editing, printing, etc. (DIY, man!!!)

I'M ACTUALLY A MEGA FAN OF BROWN RICE THESE DAYS, BUT STILL, GO WITH WHATEVER GRAIN ITERATION SPEAKS TO YOU FOR WHATEVER REASON!

honey = bee vomit

some essentials

***Nutritional Yeast-** nutritional yeast is a basically just that- a type of yeast, grown on molasses, which is high in vitamins and protein and is very nutritious. It is an excellent supplement for vegans as it is very high in vitamin B, which is not normally found in non-animal foods. It's a yellowish color and has a slightly cheesy flavor. It is a good addition to sauces, but can also be sprinkled onto foods plain. You may find it somewhat of an acquired taste, but if that's the case, try it in something like the easy mac and cheese. You will fall in love.
Nutrtional Yeast is usually available in bulk in natural foods stores or can sometimes be bought prepackaged in a tub.
**Do not try to substitute another kind of yeast for nutritional yeast! It is not the same at all. Seriously.*

***Wheat Gluten-** also referred to as vital wheat gluten, it is basically a flour derived from the protein portion of wheat that is an excellent meat substitute. Wheat gluten is combined with water, kneaded, then boiled and flavored to make seitan, a chewy, meaty, protein filled food of goodness. You can buy pre-made seitan in the form of many kinds of fake meats at natural foods stores and many vegetarian restaurant, but it's much more fun and economical to make your own.
Wheat gluten can be bought in the bulk section of most natural foods stores.

***Tofu-** I'm sure you've had tofu before (if not, then you are missing out. Like. Go make something with tofu right now). It doesn't seem like it would need much of an explanation, but if you're not really familiar with the different types of tofu, it would be useful for me to say a word about that. Tofu comes in several different types, including the most useful for our purposes, silken and extra firm. Silken tofu is soft and useful for blending (as in the broccoli soup recipe) and I like extra firm in recipes where it is to be used as a meat substitute (like the tofu nuggets).

5 **THE BaSICS** ↓ ♡

BASIC WHITE SAUCE

This sauce gets used over and over again in various forms in my cooking. ***You can add a cup (more or less) of nutritional yeast and some more salt plus whatever spices you want (onion powder and garlic salt are improvements) to make a 'cheese' sauce.***

***1 stick Vegan Margarine**
***4-6 Tbsp Flour**
*** Salt to taste**
***2-3 Cups Soy Milk (enough to achieve a thick, creamy consistency that still flows)**

1 STICK = 1/2 CUP!

Melt the margarine over medium heat and whisk in the flour. Once a paste has been formed, add the soymilk, stirring the whole time. Keep stirring over medium heat until the sauce thickens into a good consistency (creamy and thick, but not too thick).
You can always add more soymilk, but you once the soymilk has been added, you can't add more flour! So it's best to put less soymilk than you think you'll need at first.

BASIC SEITAN

*** 1-2 cups vital wheat gluten**
*** warm water (about equal to the amount of wheat gluten)**
*** soy sauce/bragg's aminos**
*** vegetable broth (with whatever else you want in it- some nutritional yeast, spices, soy sauce, ginger, whatever)**

Mix the wheat gluten and warm water and knead until it becomes a consistent texture. You can also add the soy sauce/braggs/nut. Yeast in at this point if you want.
Run under cold water, and keep kneading, until the water runs clear. If pieces start falling off, just stick them back onto the big chunk.
Meanwhile, prepare about a gallon of water with veggie broth and whatever else you want in it for flavor.
Cut seitan into finger-sized chunks (they'll grow in the broth) and boil in a covered pot for at least an hour.
Hoo-ray!

↑ (Creepy)

BROCCOLI SOUP

- **Lots of Broccoli (at least a couple of crowns)**
- **2-3 potatoes**
- **4 vegetarian boullion cubes (or other vegetable stock of your choice)**
- **1-2 cups soymilk**
- **¾ package silken tofu (other tofu will actually work too)**
- **½ large carrot (or as much as you want)**
- **Salt and Pepper to taste**
- **1 onion, chopped**
- **2 (or more) cloves garlic**
- **Margarine or Olive Oil (to sauté onions and garlic)**

> other stuff

and you know it.

Boil the water with boullion until the boullion completely dissolves (or just use premade vegetable stock). Chop potatoes and broccoli and carrot and add to veggie stock. Add the soymilk and spices as you go.
Meanwhile, sauté the onion and garlic. Once soft, add to the rest of the soup.
When all the vegetables are soft, remove from heat. Take out some of the veggies and set aside if you want a chunky soup.
Crumble in the tofu and then blend in a blender or food processor (in batches) on `GRIND` until the soup is creamy and…soupy.
Add back in the chunky veggies if you took them out to begin with.
Eat it! Yum!

*Ok, I *know* this sounds kind of weird and gross.

It isn't. I've introduced so

many friends to it who thought the same thing and they love it now.

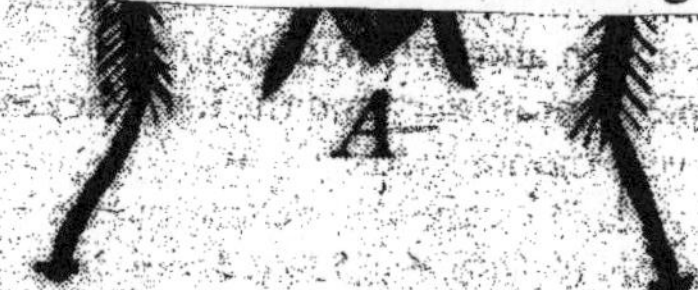

Give it a try.

POTATO CASSEROLE IS ONE OF MY FAMILY'S SPECIALTIES, PASSED DOWN THROUGH THE GENERATIONS. IF YOU'RE LOOKING FOR SOME SERIOUS STICK-TO-YOUR-RIBS COMFORT FOOD, LOOK NO FURTHER!

POTATO CASSEROLE

- **1 pckg. Vegan sour cream (I like tofutti)**
- **1 block soy cheese (Follow Your Heart's Vegan Gourmet mozzarella works well)**
- **1 large onion, chopped**
- **A lot of potatoes. Like, a lot. Like enough to fill up whatever giant casserole dish you have.**
- **1 pckg. Veggie dogs**
- **Salt and pepper to taste**

Peel the potatoes and slice them very thinly (a potato peeler actually works well for this too. Either way it's going to take a long time).
Chop veggie dogs into bite sized pieces and grate all the soy cheese.
Mix all ingredients together (save a little soy cheese) and put in a *well oiled* casserole dish. Put remaining soy cheese on top.
Bake uncovered at 375 for about 50 minutes (or more, depending how thin your potatoes are.

7

EASY AND AMAZING MAC AND CHEESE 8

- **white sauce as described on page 5**
- **¼ cup nutritional yeast**
- **1 package macaroni, cooked according to instructions**

Make the white sauce, and add the nutritional yeast, and probably some extra salt (to taste, of course). Mix it into the macaroni.
Be amazed. Feed your friends.
This is an awesome potluck food.

GIVING OUR FEAR THE FINGER *The Wendy's brouha... since Mikey supposedly blew up his stomach with Pop Rock...*

Contrary to what a friend of a friend may have heard:

• McDonald's is ~~not~~ the world's largest purchaser of cow eyeballs, ~~nor do~~ their hamburgers contain worm meat. Also,

found t... the ket... restaur...

• A hum... jar of f...

neral Foods, who produced Pop ...cks, had to take out full-page ads

MY GRAMMA'S SUGAR COOKIES

- **¾ cup margarine**
- **½ cup sugar**
- **1 egg (replacer)**
- **2 tbsp. soymilk**
- ***At least* 1 ¼ cup flour**
- **1 tsp. baking powder**
- **¼ tsp. salt**
- **2 tsp. vanilla**

Beat sugar, margarine and egg replacer well. Mix dry ingredients and stir in carefully, along with vanilla and soymilk.
Roll out about ¼ inch thick. You will probably need more flour, which you'll know when you realize the dough is sticking to your rolling pin/board, etc. Add until the dough is workable and not too sticky.
Cut with a fun cookie cutter (hearts and skulls are personal favorites) and bake at 350 for about 10 minutes. SPRINKLE SUGAR ON TOP!

Mediterranean food accented by a ... demonstrates, racism, homophobia and

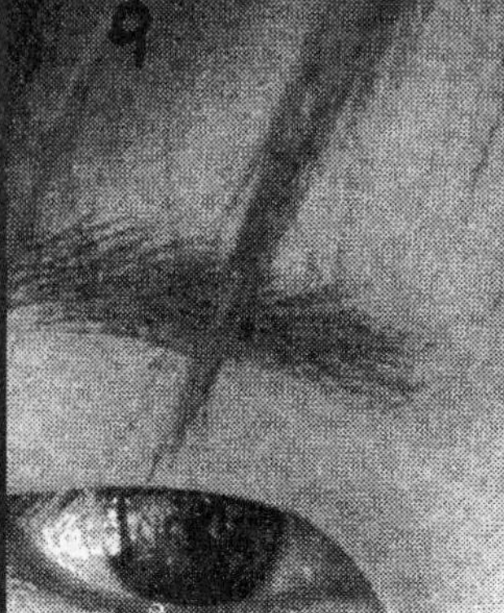

ANOTHER FAMILY FAVORITE! ARE YOU SEEING THE THEME HERE? IT'S HOT DOGS. THANK GOODNESS FOR VEGGIE DOGS.

TACO DOGS

- **small corn tortillas (as many as you want, one for each taco dog)**
- **veggie dogs (again, one for each taco dog)**
- **veggie chili (home made or store bought, it don't matta!)**
- **some grated soy cheese**
- **Additional toppings of your choosing. May well include chopped onion.**

Cut the veggie dogs down the center (making two long, flat halves). Fry up in a little bit of water or oil. Heat the tortillas and chili similarly.
Arrange the hot dog halves two to a tortilla and top with chili, soy cheese, and whatever else you want.

*This sounds weird, but I assure you, it is good. And I don't generally advocate hot dogs of any sort.

TOFU NUGGETS 10

- **1 block of extra firm tofu**
- **½ cup flour**
- **water**
- **2 tbsp or so of soy sauce (or Braggs)**
- **a splash of orange juice**
- **salt, pepper and seasonings of your choice to taste**
- **olive or other oil to fry in**

Drain the tofu and get out as much water as you can by wrapping in cheesecloth or paper towels and squeezing (but try not to crumble it). Cut into nuggety pieces and set aside.
Mix flour, soy sauce, orange juice and seasonings. Add enough water to make this a smooth –but not runny- constistency.
Dip the nuggets into the batter and fry in a thin layer of oil (or more if you want a crispier, more deep fried effect). Cook until light brown and crispy.

ate.

**Ridiculously useful tip:* If you want breaded nuggets, you can buy or make bread crumbs out of a lot of different things. Matzah meal works well, as do crushed saltines.

hy paintings and table cloths, ying Japanese lanterns and one

addition of the cream cheese created a decadent velvety texture to this

($1 extra). Unfortunately, they

**Another ridiculously useful tip:* Tofu, when frozen and thawed, gets a chewy consistency that works really well for meaty dishes like this. Try draining, cutting and then freezing it before making nuggets.

traditional breakfast and lunch

every bite held the supreme balance

paid the bill (cash or local check only), admiring

SEITAN BROCCOLI

- **1 cup prepared seitan**
- **2 ½ cups vegetable broth**
- **1 lb (ish) broccoli**
- **1 onion, chopped**
- **2 tbsp. cornstarch (or flour)**
- **2 tbsp. soy sauce**
- **onion and garlic powder**
- **1 tbsp. grated ginger**

Mix the cornstarch (or flour), onion and garlic powder, and soy sauce into 1 cup of the broth.
Heat ¼ cup broth in a wok or pan and stir fry seitan for at least five minutes.
Add broccoli and onion and stir fry another minute or two.
Add the broth mixture and ginger and cook a few more minutes, coating the ingredients well with the sauce. Score!

FRIED RICE

- **about 2 cups rice (makes a lot more once it's cooked)**
- **1 block extra firm tofu**
- **1 cup or so chopped broccoli**
- **1 carrot, thinly sliced**
- **garlic, minced. A few cloves or as much as you are into.**
- **½ onion, chopped**
- **some frozen peas. However much you want.**
- **Vegan-friendly teriyaki sauce (I advocate Soy Vey Veri Veri Teriyaki)**
- **Soy sauce**
- **Peanut or olive oil**

While you're cooking the rice, squeeze as much water as possible out of the tofu and chop into small cubes.
Cook the tofu first, in the teriyaki sauce until it is well done and chewy. You will probably need more teriyaki than you expect to, as a lot burns off.
Once the tofu is done, set it aside. Now put the steamed rice and veggies (except for the peas) in the pan (preferably a wok). Fry with a small amount of oil, teriyaki sauce, and soy sauce to taste. Once the vegetables are almost done, add the peas for just long enough for them to warm up.

*You can really put whatever vegetables you want in here, obviously. These are just ones I like. Mushrooms, peppers, snap peas, etc. might all work well.

try feeding this to omnivorous friends...

try it.

AMAZING LASAGNA

Meaty Sauce:

***15 Lasagna Noodles (one big package) Cooked According to Box Instructions**
***2 Pkg Veg. Ground Round**
***1 Large Onion Chopped**
***1 Large Jar Pasta Sauce (or make yer own!)**
***Garlic! As much as you want/can take**
***1 Tsp Basil**
***1 Tsp Oregano**
***1 Tsp Thyme**
***Black Pepper**
***Salt to taste**
***Olive Oil**

Basic White Sauce:

***Make according to recipe on page 5**

In a pot, sauté onions and garlic in olive oil for about 5-6 minutes (until soft) on medium heat. Crumble veggie ground round into pot and add the pasta sauce. Stir well. Add the herbs and black pepper. Turn the heat to low and simmer for about 30 minutes - 1 hour (the longer you leave it to simmer, the more flavorful it'll be). Stir often.

Make the white sauce when you are ready to put the lasagna together. Remember, don't try to add the flour after you've put in the soymilk and the mixture is already hot! This will ruin it!

Lightly grease a lasagna pan and place enough noodles on the bottom to cover it (this is about 4 in a large pan). Pour 1/3 of the white sauce over the noodles. Spread half of the meaty sauce on top of the white sauce and noodles. Make one more layer of noodles and use 1/3 of the white sauce and the remaining meaty sauce. Place noodles on the top and pour the remaining white sauce over the lasagna.

Cover the dish with aluminum foil and bake in a 375° oven for 30 minutes. Let cool as long as possible before serving (at least 10 minutes). This part sucks. It smells really good and you'll want to eat it, but wait! It needs some time to kinda solidify or else when you try to cut and serve it it'll be a big mess and not a piece of lasagna.

CORN BREAD

- **1 cup cornmeal**
- **1 cup flour**
- **2 tsp. baking powder**
- **2 tsp. sugar**
- **1 tsp. salt**
- **2 tbsp. oil**
- **1 ½ cups soymilk**

Preheat the oven to 350. Mix the dry ingredients, then add the soymilk and oil and mix thoroughly.
Pour into a lightly oiled pan and bake for 30 minutes.

THIS IS MY FRIEND SETH, WHO I WAS LIVING WITH DURING THESE COOKING AND ZINE-MAKING SHENANIGANS, AND A BABY GG-THE-CAT.

corn bread totally rules

my partners in culinary crime

FOR A SUPER GOOD CHILI RECIPE (IF I DO SAY SO MYSELF), SEE PAGE 46 IN MY BOOK, BAREFOOT AND IN THE KITCHEN.

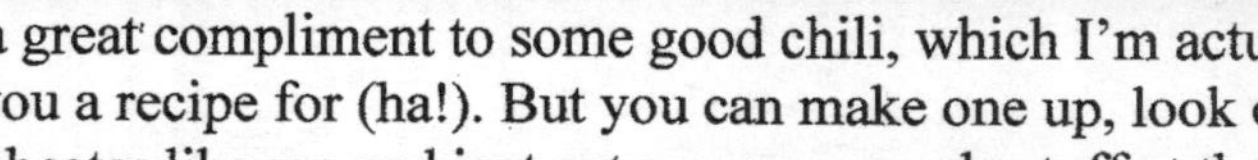

- This is a great compliment to some good chili, which I'm actually not giving you a recipe for (ha!). But you can make one up, look one up, or be a cheater like me and just get some pre-made stuff at the store. A lot of canned/packaged vegetarian chilis are really pretty good.

15

LENTIL STEW 16

- **Lentils. A bunch, several cups or so.**
- **Water. About twice as much as the volume of the lentils**
- **4 cubes of vegetable boullion (or just replace ½ or more of the water with prepared vegetable broth)**
- **a carrot or two, chopped into small pieces**
- **some frozen corn**
- **several potatoes chopped into manageable chunks**
- **1 onion, chopped**
- **olive oil**
- **1 or 2 bay leaves**
- **salt, pepper and seasonings of your choice**

Add the boullion, seasonings and bay leaves to the water and start boiling the lentils first.
Saute the onion in olive oil until soft. Add onion and the other veggies (except for corn) to the soup after the lentils have been cooking at least ½ hour.
Cook for at least an hour total and add the frozen corn right before the stew is done.

*This is awesome left over, but it may need some water added to it. The lentils soak up all the water sitting in the fridge.
*You can use either red or green lentils and also add some split yellow or green peas if you want.

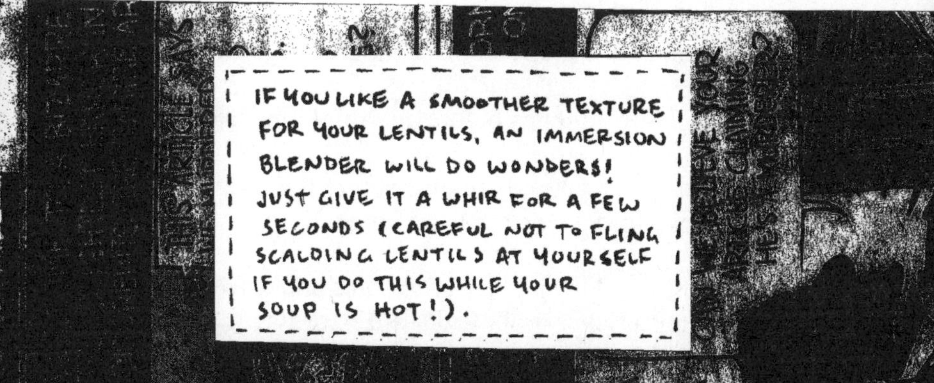

garlic can help you fight acne, yeast infections and the common cold. look it up!

VEGETABLE SOUP (one possible, and very good, variation)

* **4 cubes boullion (or other vegetable broth)**
* **lots of broccoli**
* **lots of cauliflower**
* **carrots**
* **2 or 3 potatoes**
* **1 large onion**
* **several cloves of garlic**
* **1 can of kidney beans**
* **any kind of small pasta (macaroni or tiny shells are good)**
* **salt and pepper to taste**
* **onion and garlic powder**
* **olive oil**

Chop all the vegetables to a manageable size. Boil the water and add the boullion, making sure it dissolves.
Add the veggies, potato and carrot first, since they take the longest to cook.
Add the broccoli and cauliflower a little later.
Sauté the chopped onion and garlic in olive oil until soft, then add to the broth.
Add the pasta about 10-15 minutes before you think the veggies in the soup will be done.
Add the kidney beans just a couple minutes before the soup is done (they split open and dissolve if they're in for too long).

Also: you can obviously add whatever vegetables and spices you want, including tomatoes for a richer broth and a different flavor. Some white wine is pretty ok in vegetable soup too.

FETTUCINE ALFREDO

- **1 package fettucine cooked according to instructions**
- **A couple cloves of garlic**
- **White pepper to taste**
- **1-2 Tb olive oil**
- **3 Tb or more of Vegan Parmesan Cheese**

FOR A QUICK AND EASY VEGAN PARM RECIPE, SEE PAGE 4 OF VOL. 4 (IN THIS BOOK!)

- **Basic White Sauce, prepared as described on page 5**

Prepare the white sauce while the fettucine is boiling. Mince the garlic finely and sauté it in the olive oil until soft . Add this to the white sauce, along with the vegan parmesan and pour over the cooked pasta.

You can also use vegetable broth in place of about 1/3 of the soymilk in the white sauce recipe, and add some nutritional yeast for flavor, if you'd like.

BROCCOLI RICE AU GRATIN

- **2 cups cooked rice**
- **about 1 cup steamed broccoli**
- **½ cup water or soymilk**
- **1/3 cup nutritional yeast**
- **1 tbsp. flour**
- **2 tbsp. olive oil**
- **1 tbsp. Braggs aminos**
- **1 tsp. garlic/onion salt (either, preferably both)**

Mix everything but the rice and broccoli well.
Ok, actually, you need to mix the rice and broccoli in too. But after everything else.
Stir it up. Eat it.

*Ridiculously useful tip: Cook the broccoli and rice together. It's way quicker this way. Just put your rice in the pan or rice cooker and cook until most of the water is absorbed. Put chopped broccoli on top 5-10 minutes before the rice is done and let it steam in there.

CHOCOLATE FUCKIN CHIP COOKIES

- **2 ¼ cup flour (you might need a bit more, check the consistency)**
- **1 tsp baking soda**
- **1 tsp salt**
- **1 cup vegan margarine**
- **¾ cup sugar**
- **¾ cup brown sugar**
- **1 tsp vanilla (or, alternately, cocoa powder)**
- **2 eggs' worth of egg-replacer**
- **1 ¾ cup chocolate chips**

Mix the sugars, margarine and egg replacer and beat well. Mix dry ingredients and vanilla and stir in slowly. Add the chocolate chips! Bake for 9-11 minutes at 350.

(SERIOUSLY INCREDIBLE) CINNAMON BUNS OF DOOM

soft sandwich buns (the basics):

- **2 cups soymilk**
- **¼ cup margarine or oil**
- **½ cup sugar**
- **1 ½ tsp. salt**
- **¼ cup lukewarm water**
- **2 tbsp. yeast (one of those little packets)**
- **¼ tsp. sugar**
- **about 6 cups flour**

cinnamon bun fixins:

- **margarine**
- **2 cups sugar**
- **2 tbsp. cinnamon**
- ***optional:* raisins and chopped nuts**

THIS IS FROM THE NEW FARM VEGETARIAN COOKBOOK, ONE OF MY ALL-TIME OLD SCHOOL FAVES.
FOR MY GO-TO FROSTING RECIPE, SEE PAGE 8 OF VOL. 4 (IN THIS BOOK!).

Heat the 2 cups of soymilk to scalding. Pour into a bowl containing the ¼ cup margarine, ½ cup sugar, and 1 ½ tsp. salt.
Combine in another small bowl the ¼ cup warm water, 2 tsp. yeast and ¼ tbsp. sugar. Let sit five minutes.
After the milk had cooled ad about 1 ½ cups flour and beat thoroughly.
Let rest for 5-10 minutes. Add 4 more cups of flour and beat well.
After this is added, begin to mix the dough with your hands. Add about 1 more cup of flour to create dough that is the right consistency to knead on a floured board. Knead 5 minutes, then put into a well oiled bowl and let rise for 1/2 hour.
Divide the dough in half and roll each half into a large rectangle 1/8-1/4 inch thick (keep enough flour underneath to prevent sticking).
Let dough rest about five minutes, then spread generously with margarine.
Sprinkle with 2 cups sugar and the cinnamon, and add the raisins and nuts if you're into that sort of thing.
Roll the dough up like a jelly roll and pinch at the end to seal.
Slice off 1" rolls and place on an oiled cookie sheet.
Bake at 350 for about 20 minutes.

*These seem like a ton of work (and, ok, they kind of are. It's more that they just take a really long time), but they are *so worth it*. I am serious. You must make these.

the CALIFORNIA RESTAURANT GUIDE

VEGAN + VEGAN-FRIENDLY RESTAURANTS I CAN PERSONALLY VOUCH FOR ♡

- **SIPZ FUSION CAFE**
  5501 Clairemont Mesa Blvd.
  San Diego (858) 279-3747

  11385 [Sorry WE'RE CLOSED] . Suite 100
  Powa [Sorry WE'RE CLOSED] 6-7479

- **TOFOO COM CHAY**
  388 E. Santa Clara St.
  San Jose (408) 286-6335

- **VEGAN GLORY**
  8393 Beverly Blvd.
  Los Angeles (323) 653-4900

- **GOOD KARMA**
  37 S. First Street
  San Jose (408) 294-2694

- **LANESPLITTER'S**
  203 [Sorry WE'RE CLOSED] o Av.
  Berk [Sorry WE'RE CLOSED] 5-1652

- **GRANDMA'S THAI**
  132 [Sorry WE'RE CLOSED] Blvd.
  (818 [Sorry WE'RE CLOSED]

- **VEGAN EXPRESS**
  32 [Sorry WE'RE CLOSED] a Blvd.
  LA [Sorry WE'RE CLOSED] -8837

- **ASIAN ROSE**
  154 [Sorry WE'RE CLOSED] Ave.
  (83 [Sorry WE'RE CLOSED] 23

- **GARDEN WOK**
  6117 Reseda Blvd.
  Tarzana (818) 881-8886

- **VEGGIE + TEA HOUSE**
  641 [Sorry WE'RE CLOSED] y.
  (90 [Sorry WE'RE CLOSED] 23

- **VEGGIE DELIGHT**
  1782 [Sorry WE'RE CLOSED] th St.
  (81 [Sorry WE'RE CLOSED] 7

- **REAL FOOD DAILY**
  514 [Sorry WE'RE CLOSED] ica Bl.
  (310 [Sorry WE'RE CLOSED]

- **SATURN CAFE**
  14 [Sorry WE'RE CLOSED] t.
  San [Sorry WE'RE CLOSED]) 429-8505

- **FOLLOW YOUR HEART**
  21825 Sherman Way
  Canoga Park
  (818) 340-3240

*Frost the top! Don't do it while they're too hot though or the frosting will just melt and slide off. I usually just beat margarine, a little soymilk, and powdered sugar until it is the right consistency, but you can buy or make some however you want.

recommended reading ⇩⇩⇩ ♡

the abbreviated and mostly relevant list.

THE FARM VEGETARIAN COOKBOOK

this is where the cinnamon bun recipe came from!

NO MORE PRISONS - william upski wimsatt

MAD COWBOY - howard lyman

FREE THE ANIMALS - ingrid newkirk

ISHMAEL - daniel quinn

ANIMAL LIBERATION - pete singer

THE LITTLE FOOD BOOK - craig sams

CUNT - inga muscio

SEEDS OF DECEPTION - jeffrey smith

ETHICS INTO ACTION - pete singer

DAYS OF WAR NIGHTS OF LOVE - crimethinc.

NOTES FROM THE UNDERGROUND: ZINES & THE POLITICS OF ALT. CULTURE - stephen duncombe

anything by kurt vonnegut jr.

seriously.

read these and recommend some to me →

A LITTLE SNAPSHOT OF WHAT YOUNG ASHLEY WAS FILLING HER MIND WITH AT THE TIME. SOME OF THESE ARE DATED, BUT THEY WERE FORMATIVE!

email me! with comments, suggestions or criticism:

socialobscenity@yahoo.com

You can also get in touch to get more copies, or copies of

VOLUME 2!

AND! I WOULD LOVE TO TRADE COPIES FOR YOUR ZINES... let's exchange addresses.

AND! I WOULD LOVE TO TALK TO YOU ABOUT THE PLACES ON THE RESTAURANT GUIDE!

barefoot and in the Kitchen

volume two ♡

RESISTANCE IS TASTY!

vegan recipes

for you! from me (ashley)

Innards

the obligatory introduction 2.0

Hey and welcome to volume two of Barefoot and in the Kitchen. I'm really excited to be putting out another issue this year and to have you pick this up. After all, it's all about spreading the vegan love (not to mention good food) as far and wide as possible. And, thanks to all the awesome kids in the vegan and zine communities I've encountered, I was able to spread a little bit of the love (via volume one) to several countries and a bunch of different states. Yeah!

Anyway, I want to talk about the cover of this issue, in particular my declaration that RESISTANCE IS TASTY! I mean, that's pretty self-explanatory, right? Well, for a lot of people, it's not. I've encountered so many people who don't necessarily agree with all the shit that goes on to put animal-derived foods on their plates, but just think that veganism is too much of a sacrifice to make. It's too hard, there's too much good food we're all missing out on!

Well, I and plenty of others know otherwise, and I want to help show people that animal-friendly foods can be human-friendly too. Being vegan is one of the simplest steps you can take to help end some of the most pervasive oppressive and exploitative practices in the world. And resistance to practices like animal agriculture doesn't have to be a punishment to you. It can, and should, be tasty!

So, to further emphasize my point that vegan food is fun and interesting and delicious and, you know, everything else good in the world, I've put together another batch of recipes that I hope you'll take and shape to your individual needs and preferences.

As you may have noticed in the last issue, or flipping through this one, my measurements and cooking times tend not to be exact, and I like to leave a lot of leeway for you to cook how you want to, and not just how I want you to. I think it's really important that everyone (especially vegans) get to become good enough at cooking as to be able to use inspirations or adapt recipes to suit themselves, which is what I try to do with my cooking as much as possible.

All this adapting and inspiring and whatnot leads me to a little section on page 19 called the Vegan Challenge! This is where you get to challenge me to veganize something you really love. So do it, if you feel so inclined, and make sure to challenge yourself as well. Maybe someday soon, all the amazing vegan food we're eating will be the only tactic we need in this fight for a more just world. Er, we can try anyway… Z

3

STUFFED SHELLS

- **1 box of jumbo pasta shells**
- **1 block of tofu**
- **1 large onion, chopped**
- **several cloves of garlic, chopped**
- **olive oil**
- **tomato sauce (in a jar, or homemade)**
- **salt and pepper to taste**
- **approx. ½ cup nutritional yeast**
- **1 stick vegan margarine**
- **4-6 Tbsp. flour**
- **2-3 cups soymilk**

1 STICK = 1/2 CUP!

Begin by sautéing the onion and garlic in the olive oil until both are cooked and soft.
Meanwhile, begin boiling the jumbo shells.
Then, squeeze as much water as you can out of the tofu. Once you have done this, crumble it with your hands into a large mixing bowl. Mix with the cooked onions and garlic, nutritional yeast, salt and pepper. This will be your filling.
While the shells are cooking, prepare your white sauce by melting the margarine in a medium saucepan and adding the flour to make a paste. Once this is done, add the soymilk slowly, stirring constantly until you have a creamy, thick white sauce. Add salt to taste.
Once the shells are cooked, drain them and get out your filling, your white sauce, your tomato sauce and a large greased pan to bake them on.
Fill each shell with a spoonful of the filling and place them in rows in the pan. Cover each one with about a spoonful of white sauce, and then a spoonful of tomato sauce.
Bake at 350 for 30 minutes.

BANANANANANA NUT LOAF

1 STICK = 1/2 CUP!

- **1 stick vegan margarine**
- **1 ½ cup sugar**
- **1 ½ cup bananananananas**
- **2 cups flour**
- **¾ cup soymilk**
- **1 cup chopped walnuts**
- **¾ tsp. baking soda**
- **½ tsp. baking powder**
- **½ tsp. salt**
- **1 tbsp. vanilla**

THIS BANANA BREAD IS AWARD-WINNING— AND DEFINITELY MY MOST ASKED-FOR RECIPE. A VEGANIZED VERSION OF THE RECIPE PASSED DOWN FROM MY GRANDMA TO MY MOM, IT'S EASY TO MAKE AND SO DAMN GOOD.
YOU'LL BE WAITING IMPATIENTLY FOR THOSE BANANAS YOU BOUGHT TO TURN BROWN.

Mix margarine, sugar and banananas and beat well. Mix all dry ingredients (except walnuts) and add slowly to the wet mixture. Then add soymilk and mix well.
Last, add the walnuts and mix thoroughly.
Pour into a large loaf pan and bake for 55 minutes at 350.

* Ridiculously useful tips: Use *rotten* bananananas for this recipe. Seriously. It sounds gross, but it will make your loaf so much better.
Also! A good way to find out if your loaf is done is to stick a wooden toothpick in the center. If it comes out clean, the loaf is done. If it comes out covered in wet banananana nut innards, it needs to cook a little longer.

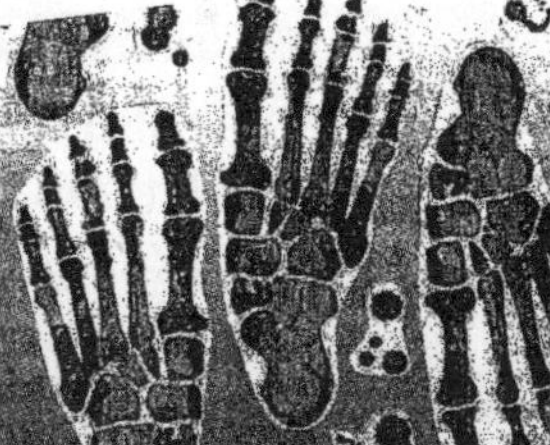

4

5

ZUCCHINI BREAD

- **¾ (small) can of pineapple, drained**
- **1 large banana, mashed**
- **1 cup oil**
- **2 cups sugar**
- **1 tbsp. cinnamon**
- **¼ tbsp. baking powder**
- **1 tbsp. vanilla**
- **1 tsp. baking soda**
- **1 tsp. salt**
- **½ cup chopped walnuts**
- **2 cups grated zucchini**
- **3 cups flour**
- **½ cup raisins (optional)**

PRESS YOUR GRATED ZUCCHINI IN SOME CHEESECLOTH OR IN BETWEEN SOME PAPER TOWELS TO GET A BIT OF THE MOISTURE OUT.

Beat margarine, sugar and banana well. Add grated zucchini, and oil. Mix together and add dry ingredients. Pour into 2 loaf pans and bake at 325 for 1 hour and 10 minutes.

*Ridiculously useful tip: As with the bananana nut loaf, a good way to find out if your loaf is done is to stick a wooden toothpick in the center. If it comes out clean, the loaf is done. If it comes out covered with moist dough, it needs to cook a little longer.

6

SPLIT PEA SOUP

- **¾ bag of dried split peas**
- **approx. 10 cups water**
- **1 cup white wine**
- **2-3 potatoes, cubed**
- **1-2 cups carrots, chopped small**
- **1 stalk celery, chopped (including top)**
- **1 large onion, chopped**
- **several cloves of garlic, minced**
- **spices to taste: salt, pepper, celery salt and a dash**
- **of Italian seasoning**

Mix that shit. Cook until the split peas become mush. Eat.

MANGO (or, you know, whatever) COMPOTE

- **2 large mangos, sliced or chopped into mid-sized cubes**
- **3 Tbsp. vegan margarine**
- **2-3 Tbsp. sugar**
- **½- 1 cup apple juice (or peach or apricot nectar)**
- **2 tsp. cinnamon**

Melt the margarine in a medium saucepan and add mango pieces. Sprinkle sugar and cinnamon over the fruit and then slowly add the juice. Cook on medium heat, stirring constantly until the fruit becomes soft and the sauce thickens into a syrup.
Serve over soy ice cream, or with granola or, you know, whatever.

*Ridiculously useful tip: You can really use kind of whatever fruit you want for this recipe. Peaches would probably work really well, as would apples, pears, or whatever.

YOU'D-NEVER-KNOW-IT-WAS-VEGAN GRAVY

- **2 Tbsp vegan margarine**
- **2 Tbsp flour**
- **1 Cup veggie broth (or boullion + water)**
- **1 Tsp-ish nutritional yeast**
- **¼ Tsp poultry seasoning**
- **a splash of soy sauce**
- **salt and pepper to taste (Do *taste* it first. You probably don't need the salt)**
- **onion and garlic powder can't hurt either, if you're into that sort of thing**

Melt the margarine over medium heat, and whisk in the flour to form a paste. Add the nutritional yeast and poultry seasoning, then the broth and soy sauce, stirring constantly. Stir over low to medium heat for several minutes until the gravy thickens to your desired consistency. It will. Just keep stirring.

*Ridiculously useful tip: Depending on what type of broth you use, you may not want to add any extra salt, or possibly even the soy sauce. Some broths are very salty, especially if it's one you've made with a boullion cube. Always taste before adding extra spices.

GARLIC MASHATATOES

- **Potatoes. A bunch of them. Like 5 or 15, depending how many people you're trying to serve.**
- **Margarine**
- **Several cloves of garlic, minced**
- **Garlic and onion powder**
- **Soymilk**
- **Olive oil (or some more margarine would work too)**
- **Salt and pepper to taste**

*None of this is exact science, in case you haven't noticed, because I don't know how many people you're trying to feed, how hungry they are, or how they like their mashatatoes.

Basically, your first task is to cut up the potatoes into small pieces, so they'll cook quickly, and boil them for about 15 minutes, until they can be cut easily with a spoon.

While the potatoes are boiling, sauté the minced garlic in the olive oil or margarine for about 5 minutes, with some salt and onion powder for taste.

Once the potatoes are cooked, drain them and return them to the pot, or to a large mixing bowl. Add the garlic, a bit more margarine, and start mashing with an electric or hand mixer. As you go, gradually add soymilk and more margarine until the potatoes are a good consistency. It's better to add too little than too much at first, so watch how much you're putting in. Add salt, pepper, onion and garlic powder to taste.

*Not exactly a tip: I like to leave the skins on my potatoes because they're better for you that way and I enjoy them. If you must, of course, you can peel them first. But they lose all their hardcore cred that way.

STUFFING

- **1 stick vegan margarine**
- **1 loaf vegan white bread**
- **1 medium onion, chopped**
- **several stalks of celery (including tops), cut into small pieces**
- **poultry seasoning**
- **thyme**
- **celery salt**
- **salt and pepper**

*Like the mashatatoes, stuffing is not an exact science. All the spices are to be added on a 'to taste' basis, so taste frequently and spice until you're satisfied.

Start by melting the margarine in a large sauce pan over medium heat. Once melted, add the celery and onion and sauté until both are soft.

While your veggies are cooking, start preparing your bread. Take a couple pieces at a time and dampen them slightly. This is so that they don't absorb all the margarine the second you crumble them into it.

Once all the bread is damp and the veggies are cooked, crumble the bread into the margarine with them. Don't make the pieces quite as small as you imagine the chunks of stuffing to be, as they will break down into smaller pieces gradually while you stir the mixture. Add the bread piece by piece, stirring constantly, and begin to add your spices.

You may need to add more spices than you think, just keep tasting as you go.

Stir with a spatula, making sure to break up all the bread pieces and creating an even mixture of bread and veggies until all the bread is bite sized and coated in margarine and seasoning. Score!

BAKED APPLES

- **4 apples (or as many as you want, 1 per person)**
- **brown sugar**
- **maple syrup**
- **cinnamon**
- **water**

Core the apples and place in a pressure cooker with a couple inches of water. Sprinkle cinnamon in the hole left by the core and pack brown sugar inside. Pour maple syrup over the top and some over the sugar in the hole.

Put the lid on the pressure cooker and cook for approximately 15 minutes, or until the apples are soft and the skins can be separated from the apples easily. Remove skins before serving or serve whole and let everyone scoop the 'meat' of their apple out themselves. Serve in a bowl with some of the sugar/syrup/juice from the pressure cooker as a sauce.

*~~Ri~~diculously useful tip: You can use whatever kind of bread you want, of course, but white bread is the bad-for-you but oh-so-good stuffing tradition.

11

CHOCOLATE CUPCAKES

- **3 Cups flour**
- **2 Cups sugar**
- **2 Cups water**
- **1 Cup oil**
- **2/3 Cup cocoa powder**
- **4 Tbsp. vinegar**
- **½ Tsp. salt**
- **2 Tsp. baking soda**

Mix all dry ingredients, and all wet ingredients separately. *Then*, mix wet and dry ingredients together and blend well. Put them in some of those cute papers in a cupcake pan and bake at 350 for 20 minutes.
Simple!

BALLS

a surprisingly appetizing dessert/snack

- **½ jar of peanut butter (about ¾ cup)**
- **½ jar of brown rice syrup (about ¾ cup)**
- **2 cups crispy rice cereal**
- **½ cup vegan chocolate chips**
- **½ Tsp vanilla**
- **½ Tsp cinnamon**

THIS RECIPE CAME FROM SOME SURELY-LONG-GONE WEBSITE BACK IN 2005, BUT THE DESCRIPTION OF THE PROCESS, AS YOU CAN PROBABLY TELL, IS ALL ME. PRETTY SURE NO ONE ELSE WOULD HAVE CHOSEN TO NAME THESE TREATS 'BALLS', EITHER.

Mix everything but the cereal together in a large mixing bowl. Once the ingredients are mixed thoroughly, add the cereal slowly and mix until it is all thoroughly coated. Wet your hands (you probably want to keep a bowl of water next to you for this) so they don't stick to the mixture and form little balls. Like, golf ball sized. Or whatever. Place the balls as you form them on a plate covered in plastic wrap or wax paper. Once you have finished, cover the balls and stick them in the refrigerator for at least ½ hour so they can solidify a little. Store them in the fridge. Love them.

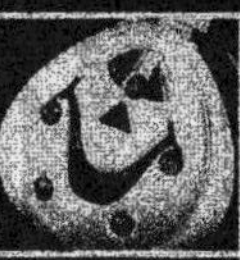

Give Squishy, CREEPY FUN!

12

TOFU SCRAMBLE

- **1 block of firm tofu, drained and dried as much as possible**
- **1 medium onion, chopped**
- **veggies of your choice (could include carrots, peppers, mushrooms, whateva!)**
- **nutritional yeast**
- **oil**
- **a splash soy sauce and/or liquid aminos**
- **a tsp. or two of turmeric**
- **a dash of: salt, pepper, onion and garlic powder** + cumin!

First, sauté the onion in the oil until it is soft and somewhat clear.
Crumble the tofu into medium sized chunks in a saucepan with a bit of oil in it. Cook the tofu (and any other veggies you may have) for a few minutes, and add the nutritional yeast, turmeric, soy sauce and other spices. Taste it as you go to see how cooked everything is and to spice it as you like.
Cook over medium heat for about ten minutes or until the tofu is cooked to your preference, making sure to stir all the time so your tofu scramble doesn't burn.

i am so serious.

this can not be overemphasized

SUPER EASY FEED-THIS-TO-NONBELIEVERS FUDGE

- 1 ¾ Cup Soymilk
- ¾ Cup Sugar
- ¾ stick of margarine
- 1 ½ Cup vegan chocolate chips (one 12 oz. bag)
- 2 tsp. vanilla
- walnuts or nuts of your choice (optional, about 1 cup)

In a medium sized saucepan, over low-medium heat, bring the soymilk and sugar to a boil. Simmer for 5-7 minutes.

In the mean time, combine all other ingredients in a mixing bowl. Once the soymilk-sugar mixture is done boiling, remove from heat and stir into the bowl with the other ingredients. Stir until chocolate chips and margarine are melted and the mixture has an even, creamy consistency. Pour into a greased 8x8 inch pan and refrigerate for several hours or overnight before slicing. If you try to do it too soon, the pieces will all stick together and not come out and it will be a big (but delicious) mess.

*Ridiculously useful tip: You can experiment with fudge recipes, adding whatever other stuff you want. A cup or so of peanut butter makes for a good variation on this recipe.

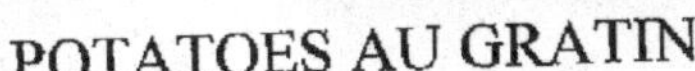

14

POTATOES AU GRATIN

*** A bunch of potatoes. Like 7 or 8 small-medium sized ones, thinly sliced.**
*** 1 stick vegan margarine**
*** 4-6 Tbsp flour**
*** 2-3 cups soymilk (enough to achieve a somewhat thick, creamy consistency)**
*** 1 large onion, chopped**
*** approx. 1 cup nutritional yeast**
*** salt and pepper to taste**

Melt the margarine on medium heat in a mid-sized sauce pan and add chopped onion. Cook until the onion is soft and somewhat clear.
Ad the flour and nutritional yeast and stir into a paste. Add soymilk slowly to the paste, stirring constantly. Keep stirring over medium heat until the mixture has turned into a thick, creamy sauce. Taste it at this point and add salt and pepper to your liking.
Mix the sauce into the sliced potatoes and cook in a thin layer in a casserole dish or even on a baking sheet at 350 for about 30 minutes.

Stuff i like that you could have thought of on your own

GARLIC PASTA

*** 1 bag of penne pasta (preferably from Trader Joe's)**
*** a lot-a lot of garlic. Like, more than you could ever think you need.**
*** olive oil**
*** salt and onion powder to taste**

Chop the garlic really small and sauté in the olive oil until mostly cooked. Add onion powder and salt to taste.
Cook the pasta.
Pour the garlic/oil mixture over the pasta.
Eat it.
Go breathe on people. Mmmmmmmmm garlic.

15

(but here's a recipe anyway...)

FRUIT AND SOYMILK

*** a bowl full of frozen fruit of your choice (mine is raspberries)**
*** soymilk**
***sugar (optional)**

Pour the soymilk over the fruit. Sprinkle on some sugar if you want, or don't, if you actually want to be healthy or something.

AGAIN WITH THE HEALTH MORALIZING! ADD SOME SUGAR IF YOU WANT. LEAVE IT OUT IF YOU DON'T WANT. FRUIT IS PRETTY GOOD EITHER WAY!

*Ridiculously useful tip: Okay, so this tip isn't actually useful at all. But there's no section for 'ridiculously *fun* tips' so here you go. If your fruit is like my raspberries and has fun little holes and crevices, make sure to pour the soymilk so it fills all of them. It will freeze inside and be extra amazing to eat. I'm serious. This is fun stuff.

BASIC SMOOTHIE

- **Juice of your choice (I like orange)**
- **Frozen fruit of your choice (I like berries, mangos and pineapple)**
- **Bananas**

Blend that shit in a blender, adding juice until you like the consistency.

*Ridiculously useful tip: You could also use soymilk in addition to or instead of juice, or add some silken tofu or peanut butter for extra flavor and protein.
You can't really fuck up a smoothie.

17 part two of the...

CALIFORNIA RESTAURANT GUIDE!

VEGAN & VEGAN-FRIENDLY RESTAURANTS I CAN PERSONALLY VOUCH FOR

♥ **SIPZ FUSION CAFE**
5501 Clairemont Mesa Blvd.
San Diego (858) 279-3747

11385 Sorry WE'RE CLOSED . Suite 100
Powa Sorry WE'RE CLOSED 86-7479

♥ **LANESPLITTER**
20 Sorry WE'RE CLOSED ablo Ave.
Be 10) 845-1652

♥ **VEGAN EXPRESS**
3217 Sorry WE'RE CLOSED Blvd.
Los A)851-8837

♥ **GARDEN WOK**
6117 Reseda Blvd.
Tarzana (818) 881-8886

♥ **VEGGIE DELIGHT**
178 Sorry WE'RE CLOSED worth St.
Gra (818) 360-3997

♥ **SATURN CAFE**
145 Sorry WE'RE CLOSED .
Santa)429-8505

♥ **DHARMA'S**
4250 Capitola Rd.
(831) 462-1717
Santa Cruz

♥ **TOFOO COM CHAY**
388 E. Santa Clara St.
San Jose (408) 286-6335

♥ **VEGAN GLORY**
8393 Beverly Blvd.
Los Angeles (323) 653-4900

♥ **GOOD KARMA**
37 S. First Street
San Jose (408) 294-2694

♥ **GRANDMA'S THAI**
1323 Sorry WE'RE CLOSED k Blvd.
Van)785-9036

♥ **ASIAN ROSE**
1547 Sorry WE'RE CLOSED Ave.
Santa)458-3023

♥ **VEGGIE & TEA HOUSE**
641 Sorry WE'RE CLOSED wy.
San I 9) 592-6323

♥ **REAL FOOD DAILY**
514 Sorry WE'RE CLOSED nica Blvd.
Santa 0) 451-7544

♥ **FOLLOW YOUR HEART**
21825 Sherman Way
Canoga Park (818) 340-3240

♥ **SOJOURNER CAFE**
134 Sorry WE'RE CLOSED Perdido St.
Santa (805) 965-7922

♥ MAGGIE MUDD
903 [Sorry WE'RE CLOSED] Ave
San F[Sorry WE'RE CLOSED]15) 641-5291

♥ LA VIE
429 [Sorry WE'RE CLOSED]
Santa [Sorry WE'RE CLOSED]) 429-ORGN

♥ BLACK CHINA BAKERY
216 Fern St. Suite A
Santa Cruz (831) 457-2068

ARE YOU FROM CALIFORNIA? HAVE YOU BEEN TO CALIFORNIA? DID I MISS YOUR FAVORITE RESTAURANT? LET ME KNOW!

RECOMMENDED READING!

DEFENDING OURSELVES - rosalind wiseman →

WHITE OLEANDER - janet fitch →

CAN'T BUY MY LOVE - jean Kilbourne →

FAT! SO? - Marilyn Wann →

THE STORY OF B - daniel quinn →

AUTOBIOGRAPHY OF A BLUE-EYED DEVIL - insa muscio →

SHIBBOLETH - penny rimbaud →

anything by kurt vonnegut, jr. still.

these books may just entertain you or just may save your life.

VEGAN CHALLENGE

Here's where I make an ass of myself trying to appease all you vegans who think you're somehow being deprived of all the good food in the world, and where I convert all your friends with that "I'd go vegan except…" crappy defeatist attitude.

No more excuses and no more dissatisfaction!

Here's where I challenge *you* to challenge *me* (see how that works?) to make your favorite recipe vegan.

Give me a food and I'll give it a try. We'll see how it works out.

EMAIL ME!
i promise to love it.
♡ socialobscenity@yahoo.com

THIS WAY YOU CAN:

- question
- compliment
- criticize
- suggest
- talk to me about books, music, politics, your zine, whatever!
- find out more about my favorite restaurants
- recommend your own
- challenge
- get more copies
- get a copy of VOLUME 1
- trade stuff w/me
- feel (and be!) totally awesome

DO IT.

YOU KNOW YOU WANT TO.

19

barefoot and in the Kitchen

vegan recipes for you!

volume three ♡

from me (ashley)

TOFU
fuckin'
Rules

Innards

the obligatory introduction 3.0

So it's been awhile, but I finally got off my ass to prepare y'all another installment of Barefoot and in the Kitchen. And I am pretty excited. I never planned to do a third volume, but then, I never planned to do a second volume either, and what can I say- the inspiration and ideas and support just keep coming.

I've had a lot of changes going on in my life since I put out the last issue, including some hard stuff and some great stuff, and I like to think that one thing that's remained stable is the happiness I get from cooking and the sense of community I feel every time I receive an email from a stranger or some stamps in the mail. I'm living in a new city now, with a new roommate (no more meat in the fridge!) and a considerably less awesome kitchen (electric stove? yep. burnt food? yeah...), but either way, there's no stopping the cooking, cos you know we've all gotta eat. I have an awesome farmer's market right near my apartment, the fresh veggies from which spawned the 'hippie shit' recipe, and I've been lucky enough to try out a bunch of new restaurants in the Bay Area, which you can find out about in the restaurant guide in the back.

In addition, I keep finding more and more ways to get this thing out to all of you, which is pretty much amazing because that's the point of it, right? Spreading the vegan

* SUCKAPUNCH DISTRO, RIP. WHAMMY INDUSTRIES, SWEET CANDY, RIP, RIP. I WAS FORTUNATE TO WORK WITH THESE FOLKS WHILE THEY WERE AROUND AND I ENCOURAGE YOU TO FIND AND SUPPORT A NEW FAVORITE ZINE DISTRO ⟶

love? Uhm, yeah. As usual, my preferred method of distribution is in person or through my own email (in back!), just because I love interacting with the people who read my zine and opening up a dialogue. Since I don't know everyone in the world, though, and it's hard to make all those contacts through random smatterings of online advertisements, I have been really fortunate to work with several great distros, including Whammy Industries (www.whammyindustries.com), Sweet Candy Distro (www.eyecandyzine.com), and AK Press (www.akpress.org). I also hear there are some great people who do tabling and include Barefoot, which is totally awesome. Remember, you all are free to copy this and distribute it to friends, just not for profit.

I guess with all this talk of distros and zines and tabling I should take a second to mention my own distro, which as of this writing is just getting started. My friend Mikey and I have created Suckapunch!* as a means for the distribution of our own work, and we hope to also start carrying stuff by our friends and all kinds of like-minded people. If you're interested in this project, drop us a line at the email address in the back!

Thanks for picking up volume three, and if you want a copy of either of the others, or to distribute them, or just to talk or whatever… email me. I will love it.

2

THAT'S STILL MAKING IT HAPPEN. AK PRESS AND, OF COURSE, MICROCOSM ARE THANKFULLY ALIVE AND THRIVING!

GRINGA TORTILLA SOUP

THE 'GRINGA' IN THIS RECIPE NAME IS TO DISABUSE YOU OF ANY EXPECTATION OF AUTHENTICITY (MY FAMILY RECIPES ARE OF THE HOT DOG AND POTATO VARIETY, REMEMBER?). IT'S STILL A DAMN GOOD SOUP.

- **1 large can tomato paste**
- **approx. 8 cups vegetable broth**
- **2 cups uncooked long grain rice**
- **2 zucchini, chopped**
- **1 ½ cups carrots, chopped small**
- **1 large onion, coarsely chopped**
- **salt, pepper, onion powder, garlic powder, chili powder, paprika, cumin and celery salt! A bunch, to taste. Taste it as you go and figure out how you like it… add about ½ tsp. at a time**
- **tortilla chips**

Combine and start boiling the broth and tomato paste. Add the rice and cook on medium heat for about ½ hour before adding other ingredients. Start adding your spices. It will probably be more than you think you need, but take it slow and taste as you go. You will probably want to use the most of salt, garlic powder, paprika and cumin.
Add the chopped veggies and cook for about another ½ hour until the are all soft and the rice is done. Crumble in tortilla chips and serve with a cilantro garnish, if you're into that.

* Ridiculously useful tip: You don't have to buy tortilla chips- you could also make your own strips for the soup by thinly slicing a couple of corn tortillas and roasting on a lightly oiled cookie sheet until they are crisp.

3

APPLE CRISP

Filling:

- **a shitload of apples (like 10)**
- **1 ½ cups water**
- **4 Tbsp. brown sugar**
- **1 Tbsp. cinnamon**

Topping:

- **3 cups of oats**
- **1 ½ cup flour**
- **2 cups sugar**
- **1 cup margarine, softened (but not melted!)**
- **pinch of salt**
- **extra cinnamon and brown sugar**

Peel and cut apples into fairly thin slices (vertically, like one of those apple slicer things does it).
Put apple slices into a large casserole dish and mix the water, brown sugar, and cinnamon to pour over them. Pour it, and set the apples aside while you make the topping.
For the topping, stir the oats, sugar and flour into the softened margarine and use your hands to mix until crumbly. Add a pinch of salt and some cinnamon. Crumble over the apples and top with a thin layer of cinnamon and brown sugar.
Bake for approx. 40 minutes at 350, until the apples are soft and the topping is crispy. Apple crisp. Get it?

* Ridiculously useful tip: You can squeeze some lemon juice onto the apple slices to keep the air from turning them brown while you prepare the topping. It also makes them taste tangy and good. Try it.

4

OATMEAL COOKIES

- **1 cup firmly packed brown sugar**
- **¾ cup vegan margarine**
- **½ cup granulated sugar**
- **½ banana**
- **¼ cup water**
- **1 tbsp. vanilla**
- **1 cup flour**
- **3 cups oats (quick cooking or old fashioned)**
- **1 tsp. salt**
- **½ tsp. baking soda**

Beat together two types of sugar, margarine, and banana. Add water and vanilla and mix well. Combine all dry ingredients first, and then slowly mix them into the wet, adding a little at a time and stirring constantly. Stick large rounded spoonfuls of dough onto a cookie sheet and bake at 350 for 11-13 minutes, until the edges are just starting to brown.

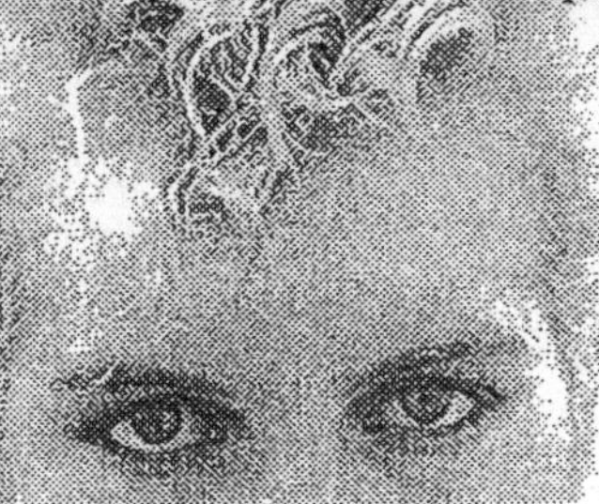

CREAMY ASPARAGUS SOUP

- **1 lb. asparagus, ends chopped off, cut into 1 inch slices**
- **1 large onion, chopped**
- **7-ish medium sized red potatoes**
- **a bunch of garlic. Like 5 cloves.**
- **½ package silken tofu**
- **6 cups vegetable broth**
- **1 Tbsp. dill**
- **1 Tbsp, nutritional yeast (optional)**
- **olive oil**
- **salt and pepper to taste**

Start by sautéing the onion and garlic with olive oil in a large pot (your soup pot) over medium heat until soft. Add the asparagus and continue to sauté until soft and almost completely cooked.

While this cooks, clean and chop your red potatoes into bite-sized pieces. Leave the skin on.

Once the asparagus, onion and garlic are cooked, add the potatoes and vegetable broth. Stir in the dill and boil until the potatoes are soft.

Once all the veggies are cooked, scoop some out, so that they won't get blended and can be added in to the creamy soup later.

Add the nutritional yeast and crumble the tofu into the remaining soup and blend in a blender or food processor until creamy. Add salt and pepper to taste.

Pour back into your big pot and add the un-blended veggies back in. Yes!

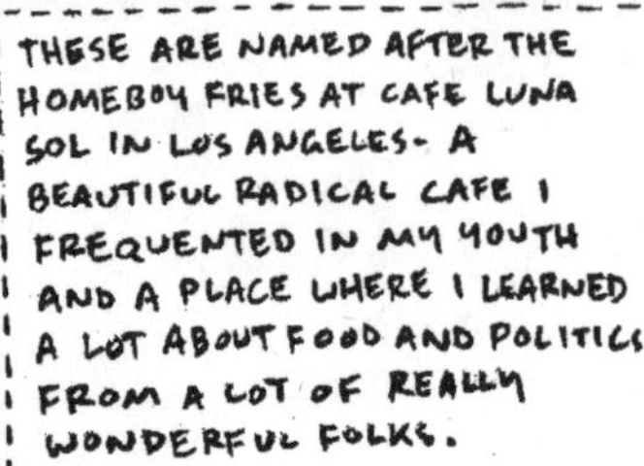

HOMEBOY FRIES

- **As many potatoes as you want (like 4)**
- **Olive oil**
- **Salt**
- **Pepper**
- **Onion powder**

Chop the potatoes (washed, but not peeled) into bite-sized cubes (maybe an inch square). Heat some oil in a medium sized saucepan. It's ok if you have too much oil- it can be drained later. Not enough is more of a problem.

Dump the potato bites into the pan with the hot (but not boiling) oil and toss until they are all coated. Sprinkle with a ton of pepper, a bunch of salt and some onion powder and cook until the potatoes are soft (about 15 minutes), always stirring. Simple! Serve with lots of ketchup.

*Ridiculously useful tip: You can spice it up with some rosemary for a more sophisticated homeboy.

7

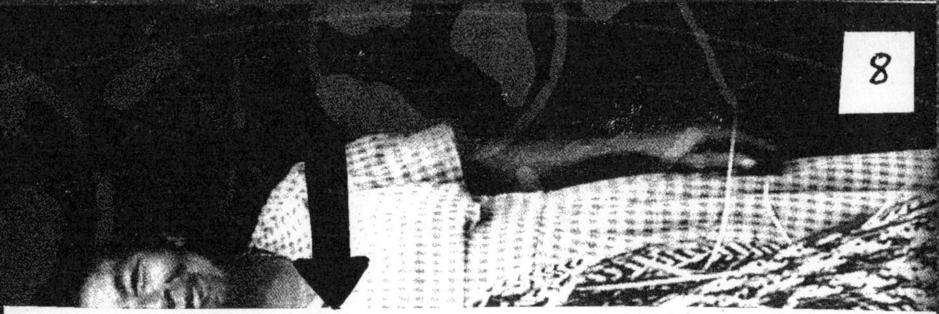

FREEDOM TOAST

- **2 Cups soymilk**
- **5 Tbsp. flour**
- **3 tsp. sugar**
- **½ tsp. cinnamon**
- **some bread (thicker slices are better)**
- **oil for frying**

Combine all ingredients (except bread and oil!) in a large mixing bowl and stir into an even consistency.

Take one slice of bread at a time and dip each side into the freedom mixture for a couple seconds, allowing it to get absorbed into the bread, but not to soak it.

Coat a frying pan with a (thin) layer of oil and heat for a minute on low-medium heat. Pan fry the bread for a few minutes on each side, until the outside becomes golden and slightly crispy.

Once cooked, sprinkle with some powdered sugar and cinnamon, or eat with margarine and syrup like that damned "French" toast with the eggs and whatnot.

Serve it with tofu scramble!

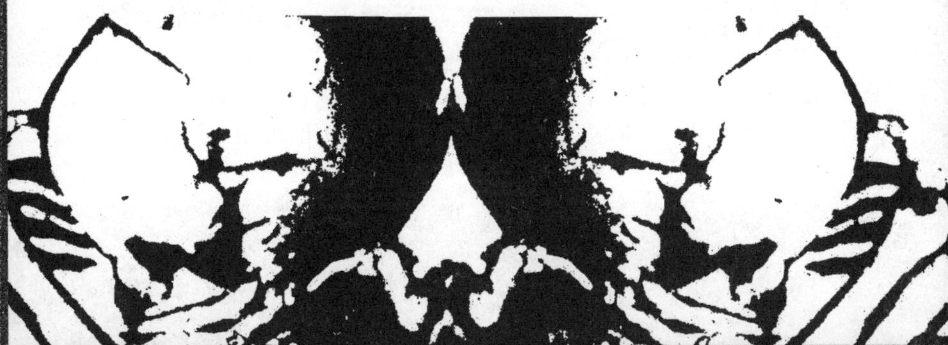

CHOCOLATE TOFU PIE

- **2 graham cracker crusts (you can make your own or buy them premade- lots are already vegan)**
- **2 packages silken tofu**
- **1 bag vegan chocolate chips**
- **3 Tbsp. brown rice syrup**
- **1 Tbsp. vanilla**

NOW THIS IS SOME OLD-SCHOOL VEGAN SHIT, ISN'T IT? BUT GUESS WHAT: TOFU PIE STILL SATISFIES.

Start by melting the chocolate chips in a double boiler (see fantastic diagram). Stir constantly to get an even texture and help the chocolate melt faster.

Once the chocolate is all melted, put in a blender or food processor along with the tofu, vanilla and brown rice syrup. Blend until it is a smooth, even consistency.

Pour into crusts and chill in the fridge for at least 2 hours, preferably longer.

* Ridiculously useful tip: This is a very basic tofu pie. You could add any number of things to make it more interesting, like peanut butter, cookies, bananas, berries, mint or whatever you want.

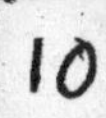

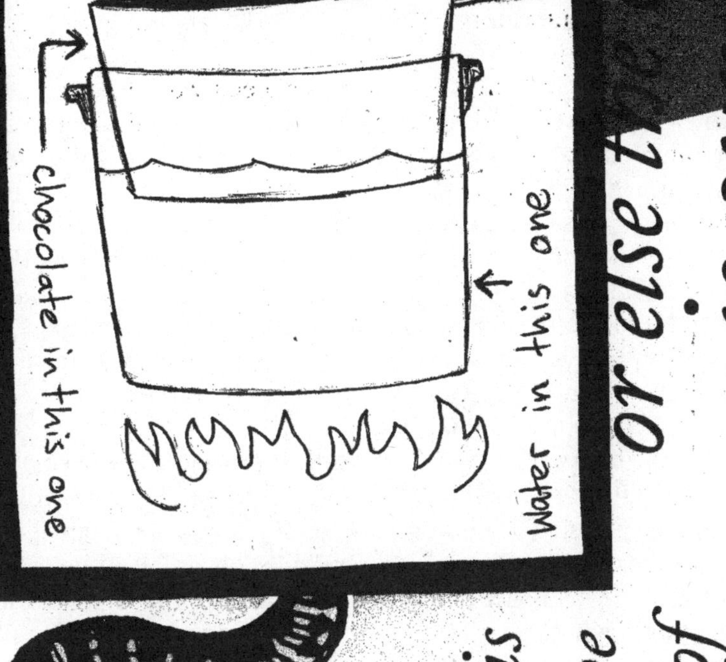

CHOCOLATE MOUSSE

Follow directions for tofu pie filling above, but add about 2 Tbsp. soymilk while you blend, to make it a bit thinner.
Chill for a couple hours and serve in a small dish with a few chocolate chips or a sprig of mint for garnish.

COCONUT AMAZINGPILES

- **2/3 Cup Soymilk**
- **2 Tbsp. granulated sugar**
- **2 Cups powdered sugar**
- **1 (14 oz.) package shredded coconut**
- **2 bags vegan chocolate chips**
- **1 tsp. vanilla**

Amazingpiles are ‘traditionally’ (ahem) made using condensed milk, which of course is filth, so the first task in this recipe is to reduce together the soymilk and the granulated sugar and make a substitute for it. To do this, mix the two and simmer on medium heat for 5 to 7 minutes, stirring constantly, until the sugar is dissolved.

Once this is done, remove from heat and, in a large mixing bowl, blend your ‘condensed’ milk, vanilla and powdered sugar, stirring until smooth. Slowly stir in the coconut and mix well. Slather the coconut mixture firmly into a well-greased 9”x13”(ish) pan and refrigerate until firm (approx. 1 hour). You want it to be as dense and firm as possible, to make the center of the amazingpiles.

Once the coconut mass is ready, take it out and cut into small 1”x2” bars. These will then be dipped (on a fork!) into the chocolate you’ve melted in a double boiler. The double boiler is explained in a fancy diagram, see? Place the chocolate dipped coconut piles on a plate or baking sheet covered in wax paper and refrigerate until the chocolate has hardened and they are ready to go. Store in the refrigerator, and, if you’re like me, don’t try to eat more than one at a time. If you can/do, let me know and I will congratulate you.

p. 10!

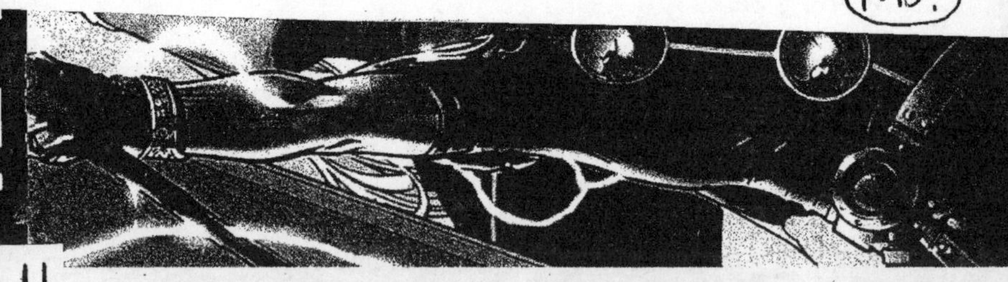

PRIMITIVIST MILKSHAKE

(a treat from Randy and Eva)

RANDY AND EVA WERE IN THE BAND GATHER, A VEGAN HxC CLASSIC.

- **Ice cream- soy, rice, whateva!**
- **Cookies**
- **Peanut butter**
- **Banana**
- **Nuts- walnuts, peanuts, almonds**
- **Syrups and crumbled things of all sorts**

Place all frostbitten ingredients into a chalice or other appropriate glass, goblet or mug. Proceed to smash with Thor's hammer (or a spoon) until you have a heterogeneous primitive milkshake of your desired consistency. Don't bother trying to use a straw. Seriously.

LEMON POPPY SEED COOKIES

- **½ Cup Margarine**
- **1 Egg (replacer)**
- **3 Tbsp. Soymilk**
- **¾ Cup Sugar**
- **2 Cups Flour**
- **1 tsp. baking powder**
- **¼ tsp. Salt**
- **¼ tsp. Almond extract**
- **½ tsp. poppyseeds**
- **zest of ½ lemon, and a squirt of juice**

Beat together the margarine, egg replacer and sugar. Add almond extract and slowly mix in all dry ingredients, adding four until the dough starts to become somewhat firm and hold together in a ball. Knead in lemon and poppyseeds.

Form balls out of about 1 large spoonful of dough at a time and flatten them onto a greased cookie sheet. Bake for 12-15 minutes at 350.

* Ridiculously useful tip: To make lemon zest, you can use any sort of tiny grater. Simply grate the outside of the lemon down to the white part before the fruit itself and toss the curly little pieces of peel into your batter.

13

'LL GO ~~TO HEAVEN~~ AND WAIT F

HIPPIE SHIT
aka Getting Back to Our Roots (and Greens)

- **Beets- red or golden, about 4 small or 2 or 3 large, thinly sliced**
- **Chard- preferably rainbow**
- **½ Onion, chopped**
- **Garlic- about three cloves, finely chopped**
- **Several small red potatoes, sliced thinly**
- **A carrot or two, cut into thin slices**
- **Olive oil**
- **Bragg's liquid aminos**
- **A sprinkle of nutritional yeast (optional-ish)**
- **A sprinkle of sesame seeds (optional-ish)**
- **Salt and pepper to taste**
- **2 cups of brown rice, cooked**

Throw all the veggies except the chard into a wok or another medium-to-large pan suitable for stir frying with a tablespoon or so of olive oil and mix well. Cook over medium heat, adding Bragg's as you go to keep the stir fry moist enough and add as much flavor as you want. Sprinkle in sesame seeds and nutritional yeast to taste, and cook everything until the beets, potatoes and carrots are all cooked and fairly soft. When your stir fry is almost done, add the chard for a couple minutes, just enough to cook it without making it overly soggy or wilted.
Pour over your rice in a large bowl and mix it all up, adding some more Bragg's, nutritional yeast, salt and pepper if you want.

I can't stand it that you're not here to hold me when I feel alone

14

PEANUT BRITTLE

- **1 1/3 Cup 'party' peanuts**
- **1 Cup Sugar**
- **½ Cup Karo Light syrup (corn syrup)**
- **1 Tbsp. Margarine**
- **1 Tsp. Vanilla**
- **1 ¼ tsp. baking soda**

Place the peanuts, sugar and karo syrup in a microwave-safe bowl (aka no metal, and nothing that might melt), and microwave for 6 minutes. This seems like a creepy long time to put something in the microwave, but don't worry about it. Take it out and stir in margarine and vanilla. Mix thoroughly and return to the microwave for another 3 minutes. Take it out and immediately add the baking soda, mixing very well. It will kind of foam up and look crazy for a second there, but that's good- this is what makes it not a solid brick.

Slather onto a greased baking sheet (with a utensil that won't melt!) as thin as possible and let cool for at least two hours. Stored in an air-tight container, this will last for 2 months.

DIRTY RICE TO FEED THE MASSES

- **4 cups rice, cooked in…**
- **5 cups veggie broth**
- **1 large onion, chopped**
- **garlic (like 5 cloves), chopped**
- **2 bell peppers, cut into slices**
- **1 can black beans**
- **1 can kidney beans**
- **¾ cup TVP (textured vegetable protein), soaked to soften**
- **2/3 can of tomato sauce**
- **½ tsp. thyme (or more)**
- **½ tsp. garlic powder**
- **a splash of soy sauce**
- **a pinch of nutritional yeast**
- **olive oil, for stir frying**
- **salt and pepper to taste**

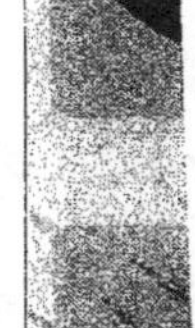

Start by chopping all your vegetables and starting your rice and veggie broth in a rice cooker (or pot, or whatever). Heat up a little bit of oil in a large pan like a wok, and stir fry together the onion, garlic and bell peppers until they are cooked to your liking. Add in the TVP, along with all the beans and the tomato sauce. Mix in your spices (and soy sauce, etc.) and keep stirring until it is all mixed and hot.

Once the rice and the 'dirty' stir fry slop sauce are both done, mix them together and feed tons of people. Or a couple really hungry ones.

s signif

gacie

EA

ER

Less

16

the revised and expanded

CALIFORNIA RESTAURANT GUIDE part III

- **TOFOO COM CHAY**
  388 E. Santa Clara St.
  San Jose (408) 286-6335

- **SATURN CAFE**
  145 Sorry WE'RE CLOSED eet
  Sant 429-8505

- **LANESPLITTER**
  2033 S Sorry WE'RE CLOSED ve.
  Berkeley 1652

- **LANESPLITTER (another!)**
  4 Sorry WE'RE CLOSED aph Ave.
  Oa 653-5350

- **GOLDEN LOTUS**
  1301 Franklin St.
  Oakland (510) 893-0383

- **GOLDEN ERA**
  395 Golden Gate Ave.
  San Francisco (415) 487-8687

- **PIZZA PLAZA**
  6211 Sorry WE'RE CLOSED Avenue
  Oakla 0-1433

- **WILDFLOWER CAFE**
  1604 G. Street
  Arcata (707) 822-0360

- **VEGAN PLATE**
  11943 Ventura Blvd.
  Studio City (818) 506-9015

- **MALABAR CAFE**
  1116 Sorry WE'RE CLOSED venue
  Santa 1) 423-7906

- **GOOD KARMA ****
  37 South First St.
  San Jose (408) 294-2694

- **JUMPING MONKEY CAFE**
  418 Sorry WE'RE CLOSED eet
  Santa 466-9770

- **NABOLOM BAKERY**
  2708 Russel Street
  Berkeley (510) 845-2253

- **GREAT WALL**
  62 Sorry WE'RE CLOSED Ave.
  Oakl 658-8454

- **ENGFER PIZZA WORKS**
  537 Seabright Ave.
  Santa Cruz (831) 429-1856

- **GARDEN WOK**
  6117 Reseda Blvd.
  Tarzana (818) 881-8886

- **HERBIVORE**
  9 Sorry WE'RE CLOSED a
  San (415) 826-5657

- **HERBIVORE (again)**
  531 Sorry WE'RE CLOSED o
  San Fra 885-7133

- GRANDMA'S THAI
  1323 Sorry WE'RE CLOSED Blvd.
  Van N Sorry WE'RE CLOSED 785-9036

- REAL FOOD DAILY
  51 Sorry WE'RE CLOSED nica Blvd.
  San Sorry WE'RE CLOSED (310) 451-7544

- VEGGIE Sorry WE'RE CLOSED
  17823 Ch Sorry WE'RE CLOSED St.
  Granada Sorry WE'RE CLOSED 360-3997

- MAGGIE MUDD
  90 Sorry WE'RE CLOSED Avenue
  San Sorry WE'RE CLOSED (415) 641-5291

- LA VIE
  429 F Sorry WE'RE CLOSED t
  Santa Sorry WE'RE CLOSED 29-ORGN

- VEGGIE + TEA HOUSE
  641 Arrow Hwy.
  San Dimas (909) 592-6323

- SOJOURNER CAFE
  134 E. Sorry WE'RE CLOSED lido St.
  Santa B Sorry WE'RE CLOSED) 965-7922

- BLACK CHINA BAKERY **
  216 Fern St. Suite A
  Santa Cruz (831) 457-2068

- VEGAN GLORY
  8393 Beverly Blvd.
  Los Angeles (323) 653-4900

- HUMPHREY YOGART
  4520 Van Nuys Blvd.
  Sherman Oaks (818) 906-2490

- DHARMA'S
  4250 Capitola Road
  Capitola (831) 462-1717

- FOLLOW YOUR HEART
  21825 Sherman Way
  Canoga Park (818) 340-3240

- SIPZ FUSION CAFE
  5501 Clairemont Mesa Blvd.
  San Diego (858) 279-3747

- SIPZ (again)
  113 Sorry WE'RE CLOSED Rd. Suite 100
  Po Sorry WE'RE CLOSED 486-7479

- ARIZMENDI BAKERY
  1331 9th Avenue
  San Francisco (415) 566-3117

- ARIZMENDI OAKLAND
  3265 Lakeshore Ave.
  Oakland (510) 268-8849

- VEGAN EXPRESS *
  3217 Sorry WE'RE CLOSED Blvd.
  Los Ang Sorry WE'RE CLOSED 851-8837

* there has been some confusion surrounding some of the ingredients used by vegan express. Please see www.livingvegan.com/articles.html before deciding to eat there.

** note new addresses!

VEGAN CHALLENGE

Here's where I make an ass of myself trying to appease all you vegans who think you're somehow being deprived of all the good food in the world, and where I convert all your friends with that "I'd go vegan except…" crappy defeatist attitude.

No more excuses and no more dissatisfaction!

Here's where I challenge *you* to challenge *me* (see how that works?) to make your favorite recipe vegan.

Give me a food and I'll give it a try. We'll see how it works out.

YES! This is the vegan challenge from volume 2. It still stands. And for those of you who have contacted me about it, look forward to volume 4! Someday. I promise.

THE RECOMMENDED LIST

what the hell are these names?. Singers? authors? booksbandsmovies?. My favorite historical figures? Only you + your mad independent research skills can decipher this volume's list of shit that is awesome!

- PAUL BARIBEAU
- VALENCIA
- JOE HILL
- THE TAKE
- MARILYN WANN
- CRISTY ROAD
- SUBMISSION HOLD
- ICON A.D.

*also, I recommend the song 'bananaphone', by Raffi

LOVE A RAFFI SHOUTOUT. FLAWLESS RECOMMENDATION, PAST ASHLEY. NO NOTES.

19

CONTACT!

email me:

socialobscenity@yahoo.com

for anything related to this zine. or unrelated. whatever.

For questions about the distro, or if you want to submit something, write to ashley + mikey at:

suckapunch.distro@gmail.com

NOPE, NO LONGER! SORRY

THIS FOOTNOTE SHOULD BE AT THE BEGINNING OF THE BOOK, OR PERHAPS ON EVERY PAGE OF THE BOOK, BECAUSE IT'S TRULY NOT A FOOTNOTE. THIS IS A COOKBOOK, BUT IT'S ONE WITH POLITICS AND A SOCIAL JUSTICE ORIENTATION. THE CRITICALITY OF TYING VEGANISM AND ANIMAL RIGHTS TO OTHER STRUGGLES AGAINST OPPRESSION SHOULD NEVER BE UNDERESTIMATED OR FORGOTTEN.

✱ Hey! Remember that the struggle for animal rights isn't the only ✱ one out there- or even one that can be easily separated from others. Our fight against oppression has to encompass all forms of life, including ourselves and our friends. Teach yourself about capitalism, racism, sexism, homophobia and privilege through good books and good conversations, and keep spreading the word!

barefoot and in the Kitchen ♡

Innards

Hey, thanks for picking up this fourth volume of Barefoot and in the Kitchen. It's been awhile, eh? Sorry about that. Life has been busy, and I couldn't bring myself to write another 'obligatory introduction'. I put it off and put it off for like a year and a half. Then I just came up with a to do ~~lit~~ list for y'all instead! Because everyone could use a little guidance, right? Not you? Well then skip this part, whatever. Fine.

p.s. the introduction isn't really why this took me so long, but I had to make up some kind of excuse, didn't I?

TO DO

AH, THE BROWN RICE REDEMPTION WE'D BEEN WAITING FOR!

- FORGET EVERY BAD THING I EVER SAID ABOUT BROWN RICE
- START HAVING YOUR OWN VEGAN POTLUCKS! IT'S A GOOD WAY TO MAKE FRIENDS, EAT DELICIOUS FOOD, + SHOW EVERYONE ELSE THAT VEGANS HAVE MORE FUN
- START YOUR OWN COOKZINE! I'VE KNOWN SEVERAL PEOPLE WHO'VE DECIDED TO PUT DOWN THEIR OWN RECIPES WITH SOME FANCY (OR NOT) FORMATTING LATELY, + REALLY, I DON'T THINK THERE COULD EVER BE TOO MUCH VEGAN FOOD OR TOO MANY ZINES IN THE WORLD. SO GET ON IT.

1

- READ, GODDAMMIT! FOR THOUSANDS OF DIY, RADICAL, UNDERGROUND, ANIMAL RIGHTS, ANARCHIST, FEMINIST, FABULOUS PUBLICATIONS, VISIT:
  AK PRESS: www.akpress.org
  and **MICROCOSM**: www.microcosmpublishing.com

  (BUT YOU KNEW THAT, RIGHT?)

- SUPPORT PRISONERS ('POLITICAL' + OTHERWISE) BY WRITING LETTERS, SENDING BOOKS, ETC. (MAKE SURE TO FIND OUT WHAT YOU CAN + CANNOT SEND FIRST!)

- WRITE ME TONS OF EMAILS ABOUT YOUR FAVORITE RESTAURANTS, YOUR FAVORITE BANDS, THE WORD OF THE DAY, WHATEVER. (PLEASE DO NOT SERIOUSLY SIGN ME UP FOR ANY WORD OF THE DAY EMAILS)
  ALSO, IF YOU COMPLETE YOUR START-YOUR-OWN-COOKZINE TASK, GET IN TOUCH + SEND ME ONE! I'LL TRADE YOU OR SOMETHING.

NOW, GO! YOU'VE GOT A LOT OF WORK TO DO. OH, BUT READ THIS ZINE FIRST. ♡

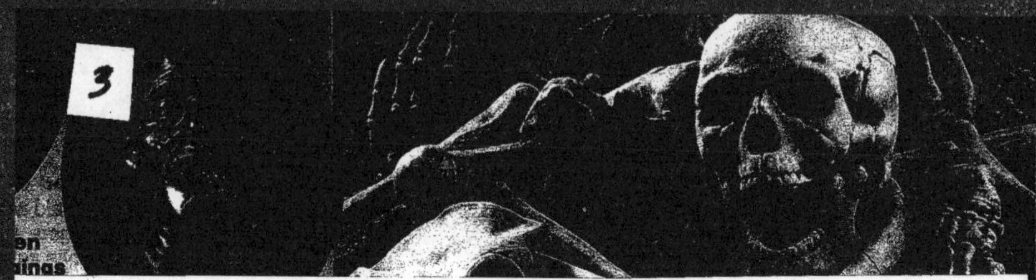

THREE BEAN SALAD WITH AVOCADO VINAIGRETTE

My friend Cassandra kind of made up the idea of mashing some avocado into salad dressing and tossing it with a bean salad for one of our potlucks. I kind of tried to eat all of it, but stupid other people kept taking their fair share. Then I decided to just make up a recipe for dressing and throw this together myself whenever I want. And not share.

- **1 can garbanzo beans (chickpeas)**
- **1 can kidney beans**
- **1 Cup cooked, chopped green beans (cold)**
- **½ avocado**
- **½ small red onion**
- **3 Tbsp. olive oil**
- **2 Tbsp. balsamic vinegar**
- **salt and pepper**
- **onion and garlic powder (optional, *I guess*)**

Drain and rinse the garbanzo and kidney beans, and combine in a large mixing bowl with the green beans.

Cut the red onion into small, thin pieces, and mix with the beans.

Take ¼ of the avocado (half of the half, get it?), or more if you like, and mix with the beans and the onion. You can cut it into slices or chunks, or mash it up. Do whatever you want. It's ok.

Now make your dressing! Mince the garlic into incredibly tiny pieces, and stick it in a glass or bowl. Mash the rest of your avocado up and put this in with the garlic, as well as the oil and vinegar. Whisk together thoroughly (I use a fork for this), until the mixture is creamy and mostly smooth. Add all the spices to taste, and then pour over the bean mixture. Quick, before it separates!

Mix it all up, and sprinkle on some more salt and pepper, as well as the onion and garlic powder if you want. Taste it. And serve that shit cold outta the fridge.

4

'KARMA' SPRINKLES

A sort-of substitute for parmesan cheese- as in, you can use it in the same situations, but don't expect it to taste the same. I'm not sure if the name of this recipe refers to the good karma you'll have for not eating real cheese, or the bad karma I'll have for blatantly ripping off a similarly-named, very expensive product that I like to eat but don't like to pay for. Wait a second, I don't think DIY is ever bad karma. Nevermind.

- **½ Cup chopped walnuts**
- **½ Cup nutritional yeast**
- **½ Tsp. salt**

Find some way to crush the shit out of the walnuts. You could use a food processor if you have one, or do it old-school style with a mortar and pestle (that would rule), or find some even more crafty DIY way to do it, like using a hammer, or the bottom of a small jar, or some kind of handle of something. Or whatever.

Once the walnuts are sufficiently pulverized, mix in the salt and nutritional yeast.

Store in an airtight container in the fridge.

NO-MEAT MEATY MEAT SAUCE

This is the super-simplest, totally easy and delicious meaty pasta sauce. You can add whatever veggies you want (I think traditional ragu contains sautéed carrots and onions), but I like my non-meat straight up, with no distractions.

- **1 15 oz. can tomato sauce**
- **+/- 5 cloves of garlic, minced**
- **½ Cup hot water**
- **¾ Cup TVP (textured vegetable protein)**
- **½ tsp. garlic powder**
- **½ tsp. onion powder**
- **1 fresh basil leaf, chopped**
- **3 tbsp. nutritional yeast**
- **2 tbsp. olive oil**
- **salt and pepper to taste**

Start by sautéing your garlic in the olive oil, stirring and cooking until soft.

In the meantime, add the hot water to your TVP in a small bowl and mix, and give it a minute to absorb and become… not so dry.

Once the garlic is cooked and the TVP is not-so-dry, add the TVP into the pan and cook it for a minute or two with the garlic, adding some of the spices at this point if you'd like.

Then, add the tomato sauce, basil and the remainder of the spices and simmer over medium heat for a good few minutes so the sauce can absorb all the good flavors and the TVP gets all saturated with everything and whatnot.

*Ridiculously useful tip: you can double or triple this recipe to use as the meat sauce in a lasagna recipe (like the one in volume one of this zine. cough. triple it. ahem.)

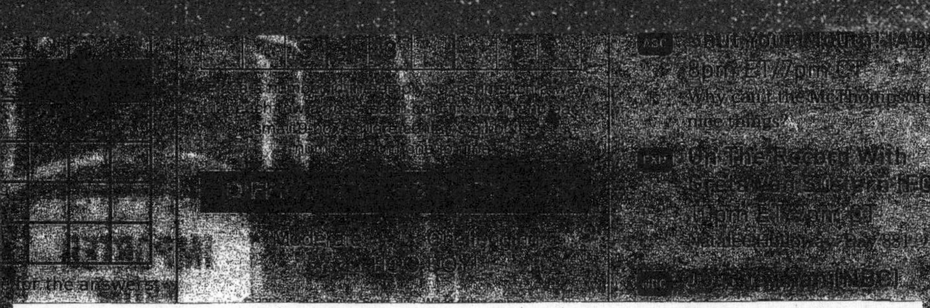

MAPLE WALNUT COOKIES

The maple walnut cookie was born as a result of my having none of the right ingredients for any other sort of cookies, and a potluck to attend in just a couple hours. They're kinda fall-apart-y (they're a party!), but they got rave reviews upon their debut. At a party.

- **¾ Cup vegan margarine**
- **½ Cup sugar**
- **1 egg-replacer**
- **½ Cup maple syrup**
- **1 Tbsp. soymilk**
- **1 Tsp. baking powder**
- **½ Tsp. salt**
- **2 Tbsp. vanilla**
- **3 ¼ Cup flour**
- **1 Cup crushed walnut pieces**
- **½ Cup chocolate chips (optional)**

Beat the margarine, sugar and egg replacer well. Then add the maple syrup, soymilk and vanilla, and mix well. In a separate container, mix the dry ingredients (except for the walnuts and chocolate chips), and then stir slowly into the wet mixture. When all that shit's thoroughly mixed, it's time to add the walnuts (and chocolate chips).

Form the dough into small, flattish cookies, and bake at 350° for about 12 minutes.

6

➤ Rupert Murdoch publicly claimed he didn't lose a single pound on the Regan-p

LEMON CAKE

This is a modified version of a vanilla cake recipe that was initially made for a birthday celebration. Vanilla cake is good, but seriously, lemon cake… it's just more interesting. Slather this with the creamy vanilla frosting whose recipe follows.

- **2 ½ Cups flour**
- **1 ½ Cup sugar**
- **1 ½ Tsp. baking soda**
- **¾ Tsp. salt**
- **1 ½ Cup warm water**
- **½ Cup vegetable oil**
- **1 Tbsp. vanilla**
- **1 ½ Tsp. vinegar**
- **zest and juice of one lemon***
- **2 8" cake pans**

Mix the flour, sugar, baking soda and salt in a large mixing bowl. Pour in the water, vanilla, oil, vinegar and lemon juice/zest, stirring until all is thoroughly mixed.

Pour half of the batter into each (greased!) cake pan, and bake for 30-40 minutes at 350°

until a toothpick can be stuck in the center and come out clean.

After both cakes are TOTALLY cool, spread frosting on the top of one, then set the other cake on top of it and frost the outside with CREAMY VANILLA FROSTING.

What's Infesting Our Houses?

*Lemon zest is basically the little shredded peel-y parts of lemon that go in baked goods. To get this, I usually just use a small grater and grate the entire outside of the lemon. There are also little 'zesting' tools though, if you're into that sort of thing and have the money/motivation to get one.

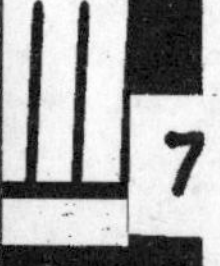

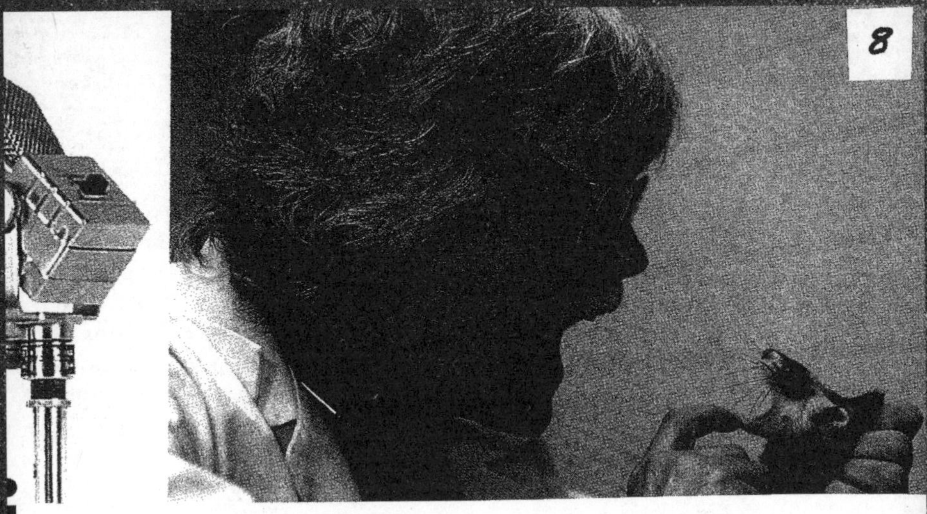

CREAMY VANILLA FROSTING

This is a good all purpose frosting, and is the recipe I probably should have included with the cinnamon buns in volume one, but I didn't, and you were on your own for awhile there, so ha. Anyway, if you don't have/can't find vegetable shortening, it's ok to substitute it with more margarine, but who wouldn't prefer a little variety, right?

- **¾ Cup vegan margarine**
- **¼ Cup vegetable shortening**
- **3 Cups powdered sugar**
- **1 Tbsp. vanilla**
- **1 Tbsp. soymilk**

Whip together the margarine and shortening for several minutes (yep, several minutes) with an electric mixer of some kind, until they start to become fluffy and no longer dense. Slowly add the powdered sugar, then the vanilla and soymilk, and beat for another minute or so.

a crockpot.

We've just left the Comedy Works, where Fitzgerald did nearly an hour of stand-up. Abuzz over having his first DVD filmed, he's spent an hour

crockpot." As Fitzgerald sometin quips on stage, "It's not a joke y but it's a good story."

FROM WHENCE HE CAME

* Ridiculously useful tip: NEVER put this on a cake/cupcake/cinnamon bun that isn't ⟶ 100% cool unless you want frosting soup (delicious, but completely impractical).

was OK? It was good?"

late mother lives on—smoki

TOFU SPREAD

This recipe was inspired by the one we used to make the tofu spread we put on bagels and sammiches at an ex-employer of mine. I have to say, other than learning to do dishes extremely efficiently, this is by far the best thing that came out of that job. Spread this shit on bagels, burgers, sammiches… whatever. Or dip French fries in it. That's the best.

- **1 block firm tofu**
- **a handful of cashews**
- **2 cloves of garlic**
- **½ tsp. salt**
- **¼ tsp. pepper**
- **½ tsp. onion powder**
- **¼ tsp. garlic powder (optional, in case you don't like garlic as much as you should)**
- **sprinkle of nutritional yeast, if you feel like it**

Basically, throw all this shit in a blender or food processor, and blend until the cashews and garlic cloves are all annihilated (or at least in really small pieces), and… that's it.

Now make some lentil burgers so you have something to spread it on.

skeletons
are
ghoulishly

SPANISH RICE

This is a recipe adapted from my mom's, which would be vegan except for all the ground beef in it. But who'd miss that anyway? If you're dead set on the meaty texture, you could throw in some TVP, but really, it doesn't need it. Stick it in burritos or eat it by itself.

- **1 medium onion, chopped**
- **½ to 1 green bell pepper, chopped**
- **2 Cups rice (uncooked)**
- **2 Cups water**
- **1 small (8 oz.) can tomato sauce**
- **½ tsp. salt**
- **½ tsp. onion powder**
- **¼ tsp. garlic powder**
- **¼ tsp. chili powder**
- **olive oil (a couple tablespoons)**

In a large pan over medium heat, sauté the onion and bell pepper in oil until almost soft.

Add the tomato sauce, then rice, water and spices, and stir.

Cover with a lid and simmer over low-medium heat until the rice is cooked, about 20-25 minutes, stirring occasionally so it doesn't stick. No one wants rice stuck all over the bottom of their damn pan, right? That's what I thought.

As always, spice to your preferences. Add more chili powder if you like some extra kick.

95 Unit Asst.

colorful burst

LENTIL BURGERS

This is a recipe my old roommate and I came up with after we found some vegan hamburger buns (and a whole bunch of other bread. And some out of date tabloid magazines…) in the trash. We needed something to fill them with (the buns, that is), and thus the burgers were born. Serve 'em with home fries, and top with pickles and ketchup (and lettuce, sprouts, tomatoes, onions… you know the drill).

- **1 ½ Cup lentils**
- **3 Cups water**
- **1 boullion cube**
- **½ onion, chopped small**
- **2 carrots, chopped small**
- **2 cloves of garlic, minced**
- **2 Tbsp. olive oil**
- **1 Cup(ish) corn (I use frozen)**
- **about 2 ½ slices of bread (dark breads work well, I think)**
- **oil to fry in**
- **Braggs liquid aminos (optional, I guess)**
- **Spices of your choosing. My choosing involves salt, pepper, garlic and onion power, nutritional yeast, maybe cumin…**
- **Buns or other bread of some sort to make sammiches on**

Start out by boiling your lentils in the water+boullion in a covered pot over medium heat until they get soft. I mean like, really soft, like you can't differentiate the individual lentils anymore and they're just like this legumey mush. This will go faster if you've soaked your lentils for a few hours first, but I never do this, so you don't have to either, if you don't want.

While the lentils are mushifying, start preparing your other veggies. Saute the onion, garlic and carrot in the olive oil until all are soft. Once the lentils and the other veggies are all cooked, mix them up, and add the corn at this point too.

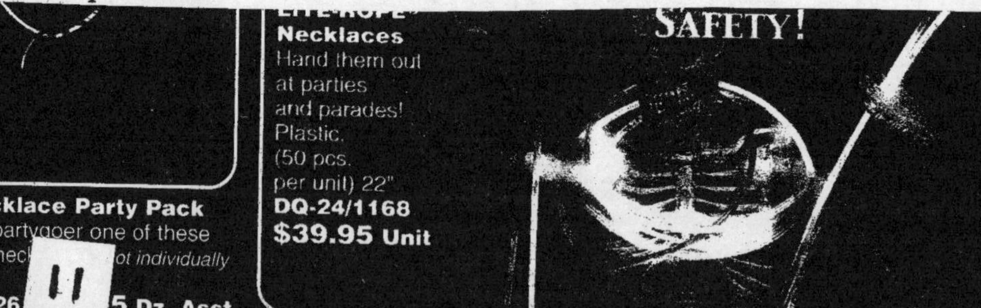

Now you can also start crumbling your bread into the lentil mixture. This is exactly what it sounds like- using your hands to crumble your bread slices into as small of crumbs as possible into the lentils so you can stir it all up and they'll assimilate into something semi-homogenous. I tend not to use the crusts for this, because they're a little harder to get to crumble right, but you can do whatever you want. Maybe you're a crust person, who knows. At this point, I start using my hands to sort of squish/kneed the mixture, because it should really be too thick to stir. As you're doing this, add your spices to taste. It's not gross to taste the lentil much before it's fried into burgers- it's actually delicious. Like I always say, taste as you go, and you're probably gonna want more spices than you think you need.

Once your mush is all flavored and mixed, it's time to fry! Put a thin layer of oil in a pan (this is where I add the Braggs actually too. I know

oil and 'water' don't mix, but sometimes I just say fuck it, you know?) and heat on medium-high heat for a minute or two. Form your burgers like you would any other- into little flattish patties that will fit in their buns. Fry for several minutes on each side, until the outside is slightly crispy, the inside is warm, and hopefully they're not falling apart. Serve 'em up!

12

13

...y, last-minute gift purchases might as well have a big sticker on them, saying "Didn't know what to get you. Waited too long. This is all they had left

CORN CHOWDA

Smart Alec's in Berkeley makes the best corn chowder ever. I think it's my favorite soup in life. After many months of trekking out there and coughing up the cash to have it served to me, I decided I was being ridiculous and that it was time to make my own. This isn't quite Smart Alec's, but it's pretty damn good, and if I can fool myself, so can you. Fool your own self, I mean. And maybe me too, I guess.

OF ALL THE RESTAURANTS THAT HAVE COME AND GONE, THIS IS ONE OF THE ONES I MISS MOST ON A DAILY BASIS. GOOD THING I CREATED THIS HOMAGE TO THEIR CORN CHOWDA WHILE THE ORIGINAL WAS STILL AROUND FOR INSPIRATION AND COMPARISON.

- **5 potatoes**
- **2 stalks of celery, chopped**
- **2 carrots, chopped**
- **1 medium onion, diced**
- **vegetable broth (several cups)**
- **¾ Cup soymilk**
- **3 cloves garlic, minced**
- **1 package frozen yellow corn**
- **olive oil (a few tablespoons to sauté the veggies)**
- **salt, pepper, dill, onion and garlic powder, and chili powder (optional. Only the chili powder, I mean)**

Saute the garlic, onion, carrots and celery together in the olive oil until all are beginning to get soft and the onion is translucent.
Meanwhile, chop the potato into bite-sized pieces and start boiling in just enough vegetable broth to cover them, plus about a half inch (does that make sense?)
When the veggies and the potatoes are all done, take about ¼ to 1/3 of each (without the broth or extra oil) and set aside, if you want your soup to be chunky.
Then, pour the rest of the veggies in their oil into the potatoes and broth, and start blending this in batches in a blender or food processor.
Once this is all done, pour your blended mixture back into a large pot to finish cooking. Add back in your un-blended veggies, as well as the corn, and slowly add the soymilk until the soup is the consistency you want it. Keep cooking the soup over medium heat to cook the corn and make it all cohesive while you add the spices. Spice the soup to taste (keep tasting it!), putting an emphasis on the salt, pepper and most of all dill. Keep stirring, tasting, and spicing until it has a good consistency and flavor.

cider and cashews, too.

*Ridiculously useful tip: As an alternative to pre-made broth, you can cover the potatoes with water and add one or two vegetable boullion cubes in order to make a broth that way.

SHEPHERD'S PIE

I have to admit, I've never eaten 'real' shepherd's pie, with the meat and whatnot. This is neither an apology nor an excuse though. Actually, maybe it is an excuse. An excuse for how delicious this vegan version is.

- **3 Cups frozen mixed veggies (I like the kind that comes with corn, carrots, peas and green beans or lima beans)**
- **1 ½ Cups (one 12 oz. package) fake meaty crumbles**
- **½ Cup margarine**
- **1 ½ Cup vegetable broth**
- **3 Tbsp. flour**
- **1 small onion, diced**
- **3 cloves garlic, minced**
- **3-4 potatoes (I leave the skins on)**
- **2 (more) Tbsp. margarine**
- **2/3 Cup soymilk**
- **salt and pepper to taste**
- **dash of nutritional yeast (optional-ish)**
- **medium sized casserole pan**

Melt the ½ cup margarine in a sauce pan and sauté the onion and garlic in it. Once the onion and garlic are soft, add the flour and whisk until thoroughly mixed. Then, whisk in the vegetable broth and keep stirring over medium heat until the mixture thickens and becomes creamy. Once it's all creamy and lovely, pour over a mixture of the frozen veggies and 'meat' in the casserole pan and mix well, adding some salt and pepper as you go.

Meanwhile, chop and boil the potatoes to make mashatatoes. When they are cooked (like enough to cut them easily with a fork), mash them thoroughly- an electric mixer really works best for this- with the 2 tbsp. margarine, soymilk, and some salt and pepper.

Spread mashatatoes over meat/veg layer in the casserole pan, creating a thickish layer on top.

Sprinkle on some nutritional yeast and bake, uncovered, for 30-35 minutes at 350° until the top is a little crispy. Slop it onto a bunch of plates and feed all your friends.

(the new) CALIFORNIA

TOFOO COM CHAY
388 E. Santa Clara St.
San Jose (408) 286-6335

A shitload of mock-meats, pho, and more.
-not quite entirely vegan-

GOLDEN LOTUS
1301 Franklin Street
Oakland (510) 893-3083

Chinese with lots of mock meats, veggies, and variety.
-all vegetarian, some dairy-

SATURN CAFÉ
145 [illegible]
Sant[illegible] 505

Sorry WE'RE CLOSED

Supe[illegible] liner.
Open [illegible]
-all vegetarian, vegan friendly-

GOLDEN ERA
395 Golden Gate Ave.
San Francisco (415) 487-8687

See Golden Lotus!
-all vegetarian, some dairy-

LANESPLITTER
203[illegible]
Ber[illegible] 52

Sorry WE'RE CLOSED

Pizz[illegible] e. They make their own 'notta ricotta' cheese.
-omnivorous, vegan friendly-

WILDFLOWER CAFÉ
1604 G Street
Arcata (707) 822-0360

Decent food, one of the only veg. restaurants around.
-all veg., vegan friendly-

LANESPLITTER (again!)
479[illegible]
Oak[illegible] 0

Sorry WE'RE CLOSED

See a[illegible]
-omn[illegible] ly-

VEGAN PLATE
11943 Ventura Blvd.
Studio City (818) 506-9015

Chinese with lots of delicious combos.
-all vegan-

GOOD KARMA
37 South First Street
San Jose (408) 294-2694

From Asian to American comfort food, with lots of mock meats.
-all vegan-

VEGAN GLORY
8393 Beverly Blvd.
Los Angeles (323) 653-4900

See Vegan Plate!
-all vegan-

15

RESTAURANT GUIDE

MALABAR/ASIAN ROSE
514 Front St...
Sa... -7906
Asi... ch with
inc... mbo
plat... r a more
expensive dinner in the same
location.
-all veg., vegan friendly-

SORRY WE'RE CLOSED

NATIVE FOODS
1110 ½ Gayley Avenue
Los Angeles (310) 209-1055

Vegan 'bowls' and lots of tasty fried foods and sauces, as well as healthy stuff.
-all vegan-

CHECK OUT DONUT FARM IN OAKLAND THESE DAYS!

PIZZA PLAZA
6211...
Oakl...

Awe... ily
own...
-all veg., very vegan friendly-

SORRY WE'RE CLOSED

PEOPLE'S DONUTS/ ECLAIR BAKERY
25... ue
Be... 221

Veg... ing
over the Bay Area.
-vegan donuts, omni bakery-

SORRY WE'RE CLOSED

NABoLOM BAKERY
2708 Russel Street
Berkeley (510) 845-2253

Collectively run, rad bakery.
-omnivorous, vegan friendly-

LAYONNA'S
443 8th Street
Oakland (510) 763-5289

Vegetarian market, filled with mock meats, noodles, and more.
-all veg., mostly vegan-

JUMPING MONKEY
41...
San... 9770

Indi... w venue
and...
-all vegan-

SORRY WE'RE CLOSED

MAO'S KITCHEN
7315...
Holly... 81

Chines...
décor. ... gan
upon request.
-omnivorous, vegan friendly-

SORRY WE'RE CLOSED

BOBBY G'S PIZZA
2072 University Ave.
Berkeley (510) 665-8866

Vegan pizza, Caesar salad, etc. Friendly and accommodating.
-omnivorous, vegan friendly-

GELATERIA NAIA
21... ne
Be... 568
Ve... char
ref...
-om... friendly-

SORRY WE'RE CLOSED

16

17

MILLENNIUM

5912 College Avenue
Oakland (510) 735-9459

Please take me on a date here. I've never been because I can't afford it. I am serious.

-all vegan-

DHARMA'S

4250 Capitola Road
Capitola (831) 462-1717

Hippie veg. food with good desserts and bottled beer.

-all veg., vegan friendly-

FOLLOW YOUR HEART

21825 Sherman Way
Canoga Park (818)340-3240

Vegetarian market & restaurant. Makers of the famous 'vegan gourmet' cheese!

-all veg., vegan friendly-

SIPZ FUSION CAFÉ

5501 Clairemont Mesa Blvd.
San Diego (858) 279-3747

Mostly Asian food with a focus on mock meats, which you can also take home frozen.

-all veg., mostly vegan-

FELLINI

1401 U... ...ue
Ber... ...00

SORRY WE'RE CLOSED

Incre... ...h, good semi-... ...the time.

-omnivorous, vegan friendly-

ARIZMENDI BAKERY

1331 9th Avenue
San Francisco (415)566-3117

Collectively-run bakery with a bunch of vegan treats.

-omnivorous, vegan friendly-

ARIZMENDI OAKLAND

3265 Lakeshore Avenue
Oakland (510) 268-8849

See above!

-omnivorous, vegan friendly-

VEGAN EXPRESS

321...
Lo... ...-8837

SORRY WE'RE CLOSED

Ma... ...e all vegan. See:
www.livingvegan.com/articles.html

-supposedly all vegan-

REAL FOOD DAILY

51... ...vd.
Sa... ...1-7544

SORRY WE'RE CLOSED

Kin... ...punk kids... ...food.

-all vegan-

MAGGIE MUDD

903 Co...
San Fr... ...291

SORRY WE'RE CLOSED

Vegan... floats, ...

-omnivorous, vegan friendly-

recommendations? questions?

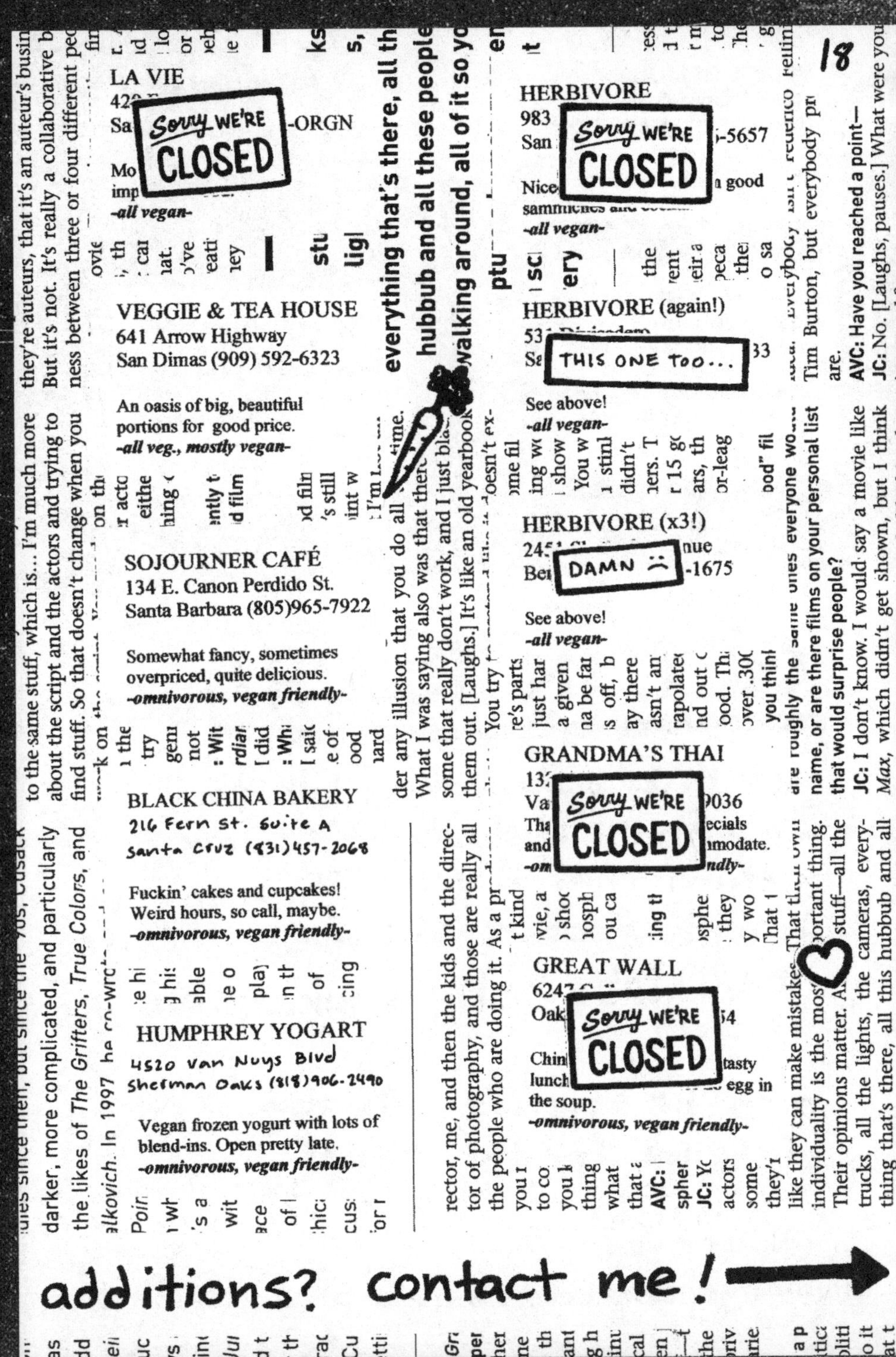

18

LA VIE
42[illegible]
Sa[illegible] -ORGN

Mo[illegible]
imp[illegible]
-all vegan-

VEGGIE & TEA HOUSE
641 Arrow Highway
San Dimas (909) 592-6323

An oasis of big, beautiful portions for good price.
-all veg., mostly vegan-

SOJOURNER CAFÉ
134 E. Canon Perdido St.
Santa Barbara (805)965-7922

Somewhat fancy, sometimes overpriced, quite delicious.
-omnivorous, vegan friendly-

BLACK CHINA BAKERY
216 Fern St. Suite A
Santa Cruz (831)457-2068

Fuckin' cakes and cupcakes! Weird hours, so call, maybe.
-omnivorous, vegan friendly-

HUMPHREY YOGART
4520 Van Nuys Blvd
Sherman Oaks (818)906-2490

Vegan frozen yogurt with lots of blend-ins. Open pretty late.
-omnivorous, vegan friendly-

HERBIVORE
983 [illegible]
San [illegible] -5657

Nice[illegible] good
-all vegan-

HERBIVORE (again!)
53[illegible]
Sa[illegible] 33

See above!
-all vegan-

HERBIVORE (x3!)
24[illegible] nue
Be[illegible] -1675

See above!
-all vegan-

GRANDMA'S THAI
13[illegible]
Va[illegible] 9036
Tha[illegible] ecials
and[illegible] mmodate.
-om[illegible] ndly-

GREAT WALL
624[illegible]
Oak[illegible] 54

Chin[illegible] tasty
lunch[illegible] egg in
the soup.
-omnivorous, vegan friendly-

additions? contact me! →

VEGGIE DELIGHT
17823 Chatsworth St.
Granada Hills (818)360-3997

See Garden Wok!
-all vegan-

GARDEN WOK
6117 Reseda Blvd.
Tarzana (818) 881-8886

Chinese with lots of mock meats and lots of variety. And nice people.
-all vegan-

ENGFER PIZZA WORKS
537 Seabright Avenue
Santa Cruz (831) 429-1856

Pizza and lots of beer, by the beach!
-omnivorous, vegan friendly-

GET IN TOUCH!

you know you wanna talk to me – about restaurants, recipes, nothing that has anything to do with food. email me:

socialobscenity@yahoo.com

also, be friends with my myspace for the remote possibility of updates. or whatever.

www.myspace.com/barefootandinthekitchen

19

MYSPACE! OH BOY! NEEDLESS TO SAY ... YOU CAN NO LONGER FIND ME ON MYSPACE.

Ashley Rowe Palafox, the author of the book *Barefoot and in the Kitchen: Vegan Recipes for You* and *Cook Your Own Fucking Life: Vegan Comfort Food to Feed Yourself and Build Community*, is a long-time zine-maker and comic-drawer. Ashley came to veganism via punk rock as a teenager in Los Angeles (before it was a vegan food destination) and majored in Community Studies at UC Santa Cruz before settling in Oakland, CA. Ashley co-founded and ran Fat Bottom Bakery from 2009 to 2014, and she has worked in fields from radical publishing to vegan food, and now the clinical laboratory.

SUBSCRIBE!

For as little as $15/month, you can support a small, independent publisher and get every book that we publish—delivered to your doorstep!

www.Microcosm.Pub/BFF

Other books about Green Self-Empowerment: